Daily Method of Operations

At the end of the day, we are accountable to
ourselves – our success is a result of what we do.
~Catherine Pulsifer~

Week of:

Activities	MONDAY	TUESDAY	WEDNESDAY	THURSDAY	FRIDAY	SATURDAY	SUNDAY
TWO NEW PEOPLE New or memory jogger people. First time or reconnect.							
TWO NEW SHARES Share story, video, invite to group or event.							
TWO FOLLOW-UPS • Is this a good time to talk? • What did you like best about the info shared? • Are you ready to get started?							
TWO CUSTOMERS Customer Care Check-ins Add to FB group Referral Program							
SOCIAL MEDIA Post and comment (on your feed and in groups) 80/20 rule							
PERSONAL GROWTH Books, Audios, training call/zooms.							
TWO TEAM Connections and help with NEXT STEPS. Set up 3-way calls or zoom.							
Although the following may not occur daily, the more frequent they occur, the faster you will grow.							
EVENTS Promote an event. Host, attend, and/or present at an event.							
3-WAY CALL ZOOM Schedule, support, connect							
PRESENTING Your story, company, product, business							

Week of ____________

If you can imagine it, you can achieve it; if you can dream it, you can become it. –William Arthur Ward

If you can imagine it, you can achieve it; if you can dream it, you can become it. –William Arthur Ward
If you can imagine it, you can achieve it; if you can dream it, you can become it. –William Arthur Ward
If you can imagine it, you can achieve it; if you can dream it, you can become it. –William Arthur Ward

Go confidently in the direction of your dreams. Live the life you have imagined. – Henry David Thoreau

Go confidently in the direction of your dreams. Live the life you have imagined. – Henry David Thoreau
Go confidently in the direction of your dreams. Live the life you have imagined. – Henry David Thoreau
Go confidently in the direction of your dreams. Live the life you have imagined. – Henry David Thoreau

Social Media ContentPlanner

Sunday	Monday	Tuesday	Wednesday	Thursday	Friday	Saturday

Week of:

Activities	MONDAY	TUESDAY	WEDNESDAY	THURSDAY	FRIDAY	SATURDAY	SUNDAY
TWO NEW PEOPLE New or memory jogger people. First time or reconnect.							
TWO NEW SHARES Share story, video, invite to group or event.							
TWO FOLLOW-UPS • Is this a good time to talk? • What did you like best about the info shared? • Are you ready to get started?							
TWO CUSTOMERS Customer Care Check-ins Add to FB group Referral Program							
SOCIAL MEDIA Post and comment (on your feed and in groups) 80/20 rule							
PERSONAL GROWTH Books, Audios, training call/zooms.							
TWO TEAM Connections and help with NEXT STEPS. Set up 3-way calls or zoom.							
Although the following may not occur daily, the more frequent they occur, the faster you will grow.							
EVENTS Promote an event. Host, attend, and/or present at an event.							
3-WAY CALL ZOOM Schedule, support, connect							
PRESENTING Your story, company, product, business							

Week of ___________

If you can imagine it, you can achieve it; if you can dream it, you can become it. —William Arthur Ward

If you can imagine it, you can achieve it; if you can dream it, you can become it. —William Arthur Ward

If you can imagine it, you can achieve it; if you can dream it, you can become it. —William Arthur Ward

If you can imagine it, you can achieve it; if you can dream it, you can become it. —William Arthur Ward

Go confidently in the direction of your dreams. Live the life you have imagined. – Henry David Thoreau

Go confidently in the direction of your dreams. Live the life you have imagined. – Henry David Thoreau

Go confidently in the direction of your dreams. Live the life you have imagined. – Henry David Thoreau

Go confidently in the direction of your dreams. Live the life you have imagined. – Henry David Thoreau

Social Media Content Planner

Sunday	Monday	Tuesday	Wednesday	Thursday	Friday	Saturday

Week of:

Activities	MONDAY	TUESDAY	WEDNESDAY	THURSDAY	FRIDAY	SATURDAY	SUNDAY
TWO NEW PEOPLE New or memory jogger people. First time or reconnect.							
TWO NEW SHARES Share story, video, invite to group or event.							
TWO FOLLOW-UPS • Is this a good time to talk? • What did you like best about the info shared? • Are you ready to get started?							
TWO CUSTOMERS Customer Care Check-ins Add to FB group Referral Program							
SOCIAL MEDIA Post and comment (on your feed and in groups) 80/20 rule							
PERSONAL GROWTH Books, Audios, training call/zooms.							
TWO TEAM Connections and help with NEXT STEPS. Set up 3-way calls or zoom.							
Although the following may not occur daily, the more frequent they occur, the faster you will grow.							
EVENTS Promote an event. Host, attend, and/or present at an event.							
3-WAY CALL ZOOM Schedule, support, connect							
PRESENTING Your story, company, product, business							

Week of ____________

If you can imagine it, you can achieve it; if you can dream it, you can become it. –William Arthur Ward

If you can imagine it, you can achieve it; if you can dream it, you can become it. –William Arthur Ward

If you can imagine it, you can achieve it; if you can dream it, you can become it. –William Arthur Ward

If you can imagine it, you can achieve it; if you can dream it, you can become it. –William Arthur Ward

Go confidently in the direction of your dreams. Live the life you have imagined. – Henry David Thoreau

Go confidently in the direction of your dreams. Live the life you have imagined. – Henry David Thoreau

Go confidently in the direction of your dreams. Live the life you have imagined. – Henry David Thoreau

Go confidently in the direction of your dreams. Live the life you have imagined. – Henry David Thoreau

Social Media ContentPlanner

Sunday	Monday	Tuesday	Wednesday	Thursday	Friday	Saturday

Week of:

Activities	MONDAY	TUESDAY	WEDNESDAY	THURSDAY	FRIDAY	SATURDAY	SUNDAY
TWO NEW PEOPLE New or memory jogger people. First time or reconnect.							
TWO NEW SHARES Share story, video, invite to group or event.							
TWO FOLLOW-UPS • Is this a good time to talk? • What did you like best about the info shared? • Are you ready to get started?							
TWO CUSTOMERS Customer Care Check-ins Add to FB group Referral Program							
SOCIAL MEDIA Post and comment (on your feed and in groups) 80/20 rule							
PERSONAL GROWTH Books, Audios, training call/zooms.							
TWO TEAM Connections and help with NEXT STEPS. Set up 3-way calls or zoom.							
Although the following may not occur daily, the more frequent they occur, the faster you will grow.							
EVENTS Promote an event. Host, attend, and/or present at an event.							
3-WAY CALL ZOOM Schedule, support, connect							
PRESENTING Your story, company, product, business							

Week of ____________

If you can imagine it, you can achieve it; if you can dream it, you can become it. —William Arthur Ward
If you can imagine it, you can achieve it; if you can dream it, you can become it. —William Arthur Ward
If you can imagine it, you can achieve it; if you can dream it, you can become it. —William Arthur Ward
If you can imagine it, you can achieve it; if you can dream it, you can become it. —William Arthur Ward

Go confidently in the direction of your dreams. Live the life you have imagined. – Henry David Thoreau
Go confidently in the direction of your dreams. Live the life you have imagined. – Henry David Thoreau
Go confidently in the direction of your dreams. Live the life you have imagined. – Henry David Thoreau
Go confidently in the direction of your dreams. Live the life you have imagined. – Henry David Thoreau

Social Media Content Planner

Sunday	Monday	Tuesday	Wednesday	Thursday	Friday	Saturday

Week of:

Activities	MONDAY	TUESDAY	WEDNESDAY	THURSDAY	FRIDAY	SATURDAY	SUNDAY
TWO NEW PEOPLE New or memory jogger people. First time or reconnect.							
TWO NEW SHARES Share story, video, invite to group or event.							
TWO FOLLOW-UPS • Is this a good time to talk? • What did you like best about the info shared? • Are you ready to get started?							
TWO CUSTOMERS Customer Care Check-ins Add to FB group Referral Program							
SOCIAL MEDIA Post and comment (on your feed and in groups) 80/20 rule							
PERSONAL GROWTH Books, Audios, training call/zooms.							
TWO TEAM Connections and help with NEXT STEPS. Set up 3-way calls or zoom.							
Although the following may not occur daily, the more frequent they occur, the faster you will grow.							
EVENTS Promote an event. Host, attend, and/or present at an event.							
3-WAY CALL ZOOM Schedule, support, connect							
PRESENTING Your story, company, product, business							

Week of ___________

If you can imagine it, you can achieve it; if you can dream it, you can become it. –William Arthur Ward

If you can imagine it, you can achieve it; if you can dream it, you can become it. –William Arthur Ward

If you can imagine it, you can achieve it; if you can dream it, you can become it. –William Arthur Ward

If you can imagine it, you can achieve it; if you can dream it, you can become it. –William Arthur Ward

Go confidently in the direction of your dreams. Live the life you have imagined. – Henry David Thoreau

Go confidently in the direction of your dreams. Live the life you have imagined. – Henry David Thoreau

Go confidently in the direction of your dreams. Live the life you have imagined. – Henry David Thoreau

Go confidently in the direction of your dreams. Live the life you have imagined. – Henry David Thoreau

Social Media ContentPlanner

Sunday	Monday	Tuesday	Wednesday	Thursday	Friday	Saturday

Week of:

Activities	MONDAY	TUESDAY	WEDNESDAY	THURSDAY	FRIDAY	SATURDAY	SUNDAY
TWO NEW PEOPLE New or memory jogger people. First time or reconnect.							
TWO NEW SHARES Share story, video, invite to group or event.							
TWO FOLLOW-UPS • Is this a good time to talk? • What did you like best about the info shared? • Are you ready to get started?							
TWO CUSTOMERS Customer Care Check-ins Add to FB group Referral Program							
SOCIAL MEDIA Post and comment (on your feed and in groups) 80/20 rule							
PERSONAL GROWTH Books, Audios, training call/zooms.							
TWO TEAM Connections and help with NEXT STEPS. Set up 3-way calls or zoom.							
Although the following may not occur daily, the more frequent they occur, the faster you will grow.							
EVENTS Promote an event. Host, attend, and/or present at an event.							
3-WAY CALL ZOOM Schedule, support, connect							
PRESENTING Your story, company, product, business							

Week of ____________

If you can imagine it, you can achieve it; if you can dream it, you can become it. –William Arthur Ward

If you can imagine it, you can achieve it; if you can dream it, you can become it. –William Arthur Ward
If you can imagine it, you can achieve it; if you can dream it, you can become it. –William Arthur Ward
If you can imagine it, you can achieve it; if you can dream it, you can become it. –William Arthur Ward

Go confidently in the direction of your dreams. Live the life you have imagined. – Henry David Thoreau

Go confidently in the direction of your dreams. Live the life you have imagined. – Henry David Thoreau
Go confidently in the direction of your dreams. Live the life you have imagined. – Henry David Thoreau
Go confidently in the direction of your dreams. Live the life you have imagined. – Henry David Thoreau

Social Media Content Planner

Sunday	Monday	Tuesday	Wednesday	Thursday	Friday	Saturday

Week of:

Activities	MONDAY	TUESDAY	WEDNESDAY	THURSDAY	FRIDAY	SATURDAY	SUNDAY
TWO NEW PEOPLE New or memory jogger people. First time or reconnect.							
TWO NEW SHARES Share story, video, invite to group or event.							
TWO FOLLOW-UPS • Is this a good time to talk? • What did you like best about the info shared? • Are you ready to get started?							
TWO CUSTOMERS Customer Care Check-ins Add to FB group Referral Program							
SOCIAL MEDIA Post and comment (on your feed and in groups) 80/20 rule							
PERSONAL GROWTH Books, Audios, training call/zooms.							
TWO TEAM Connections and help with NEXT STEPS. Set up 3-way calls or zoom.							
Although the following may not occur daily, the more frequent they occur, the faster you will grow.							
EVENTS Promote an event. Host, attend, and/or present at an event.							
3-WAY CALL ZOOM Schedule, support, connect							
PRESENTING Your story, company, product, business							

Week of ______________

If you can imagine it, you can achieve it; if you can dream it, you can become it. –William Arthur Ward

If you can imagine it, you can achieve it; if you can dream it, you can become it. –William Arthur Ward

If you can imagine it, you can achieve it; if you can dream it, you can become it. –William Arthur Ward

If you can imagine it, you can achieve it; if you can dream it, you can become it. –William Arthur Ward

Go confidently in the direction of your dreams. Live the life you have imagined. – Henry David Thoreau

Go confidently in the direction of your dreams. Live the life you have imagined. – Henry David Thoreau

Go confidently in the direction of your dreams. Live the life you have imagined. – Henry David Thoreau

Go confidently in the direction of your dreams. Live the life you have imagined. – Henry David Thoreau

Social Media ContentPlanner

Sunday	Monday	Tuesday	Wednesday	Thursday	Friday	Saturday

Week of:

Activities	MONDAY	TUESDAY	WEDNESDAY	THURSDAY	FRIDAY	SATURDAY	SUNDAY
TWO NEW PEOPLE New or memory jogger people. First time or reconnect.							
TWO NEW SHARES Share story, video, invite to group or event.							
TWO FOLLOW-UPS • Is this a good time to talk? • What did you like best about the info shared? • Are you ready to get started?							
TWO CUSTOMERS Customer Care Check-ins Add to FB group Referral Program							
SOCIAL MEDIA Post and comment (on your feed and in groups) 80/20 rule							
PERSONAL GROWTH Books, Audios, training call/zooms.							
TWO TEAM Connections and help with NEXT STEPS. Set up 3-way calls or zoom.							
Although the following may not occur daily, the more frequent they occur, the faster you will grow.							
EVENTS Promote an event. Host, attend, and/or present at an event.							
3-WAY CALL ZOOM Schedule, support, connect							
PRESENTING Your story, company, product, business							

Week of ______________

If you can imagine it, you can achieve it; if you can dream it, you can become it. – William Arthur Ward

If you can imagine it, you can achieve it; if you can dream it, you can become it. – William Arthur Ward

If you can imagine it, you can achieve it; if you can dream it, you can become it. – William Arthur Ward

If you can imagine it, you can achieve it; if you can dream it, you can become it. – William Arthur Ward

Go confidently in the direction of your dreams. Live the life you have imagined. – Henry David Thoreau

Go confidently in the direction of your dreams. Live the life you have imagined. – Henry David Thoreau

Go confidently in the direction of your dreams. Live the life you have imagined. – Henry David Thoreau

Go confidently in the direction of your dreams. Live the life you have imagined. – Henry David Thoreau

Social Media Content Planner

Sunday	Monday	Tuesday	Wednesday	Thursday	Friday	Saturday

Week of:

Activities	MONDAY	TUESDAY	WEDNESDAY	THURSDAY	FRIDAY	SATURDAY	SUNDAY
TWO NEW PEOPLE New or memory jogger people. First time or reconnect.							
TWO NEW SHARES Share story, video, invite to group or event.							
TWO FOLLOW-UPS • Is this a good time to talk? • What did you like best about the info shared? • Are you ready to get started?							
TWO CUSTOMERS Customer Care Check-ins Add to FB group Referral Program							
SOCIAL MEDIA Post and comment (on your feed and in groups) 80/20 rule							
PERSONAL GROWTH Books, Audios, training call/zooms.							
TWO TEAM Connections and help with NEXT STEPS. Set up 3-way calls or zoom.							
Although the following may not occur daily, the more frequent they occur, the faster you will grow.							
EVENTS Promote an event. Host, attend, and/or present at an event.							
3-WAY CALL ZOOM Schedule, support, connect							
PRESENTING Your story, company, product, business							

Week of ____________

If you can imagine it, you can achieve it; if you can dream it, you can become it. –William Arthur Ward

If you can imagine it, you can achieve it; if you can dream it, you can become it. –William Arthur Ward
If you can imagine it, you can achieve it; if you can dream it, you can become it. –William Arthur Ward
If you can imagine it, you can achieve it; if you can dream it, you can become it. –William Arthur Ward

Go confidently in the direction of your dreams. Live the life you have imagined. – Henry David Thoreau

Go confidently in the direction of your dreams. Live the life you have imagined. – Henry David Thoreau
Go confidently in the direction of your dreams. Live the life you have imagined. – Henry David Thoreau
Go confidently in the direction of your dreams. Live the life you have imagined. – Henry David Thoreau

Social Media ContentPlanner

Sunday	Monday	Tuesday	Wednesday	Thursday	Friday	Saturday

Week of:

Activities	MONDAY	TUESDAY	WEDNESDAY	THURSDAY	FRIDAY	SATURDAY	SUNDAY
TWO NEW PEOPLE New or memory jogger people. First time or reconnect.							
TWO NEW SHARES Share story, video, invite to group or event.							
TWO FOLLOW-UPS • Is this a good time to talk? • What did you like best about the info shared? • Are you ready to get started?							
TWO CUSTOMERS Customer Care Check-ins Add to FB group Referral Program							
SOCIAL MEDIA Post and comment (on your feed and in groups) 80/20 rule							
PERSONAL GROWTH Books, Audios, training call/zooms.							
TWO TEAM Connections and help with NEXT STEPS. Set up 3-way calls or zoom.							
Although the following may not occur daily, the more frequent they occur, the faster you will grow.							
EVENTS Promote an event. Host, attend, and/or present at an event.							
3-WAY CALL ZOOM Schedule, support, connect							
PRESENTING Your story, company, product, business							

Week of ______________

If you can imagine it, you can achieve it; if you can dream it, you can become it. —William Arthur Ward
If you can imagine it, you can achieve it; if you can dream it, you can become it. —William Arthur Ward
If you can imagine it, you can achieve it; if you can dream it, you can become it. —William Arthur Ward
If you can imagine it, you can achieve it; if you can dream it, you can become it. —William Arthur Ward

Go confidently in the direction of your dreams. Live the life you have imagined. – Henry David Thoreau
Go confidently in the direction of your dreams. Live the life you have imagined. – Henry David Thoreau
Go confidently in the direction of your dreams. Live the life you have imagined. – Henry David Thoreau
Go confidently in the direction of your dreams. Live the life you have imagined. – Henry David Thoreau

Social Media Content Planner

Sunday	Monday	Tuesday	Wednesday	Thursday	Friday	Saturday

Week of:

Activities	MONDAY	TUESDAY	WEDNESDAY	THURSDAY	FRIDAY	SATURDAY	SUNDAY
TWO NEW PEOPLE New or memory jogger people. First time or reconnect.							
TWO NEW SHARES Share story, video, invite to group or event.							
TWO FOLLOW-UPS • Is this a good time to talk? • What did you like best about the info shared? • Are you ready to get started?							
TWO CUSTOMERS Customer Care Check-ins Add to FB group Referral Program							
SOCIAL MEDIA Post and comment (on your feed and in groups) 80/20 rule							
PERSONAL GROWTH Books, Audios, training call/zooms.							
TWO TEAM Connections and help with NEXT STEPS. Set up 3-way calls or zoom.							
Although the following may not occur daily, the more frequent they occur, the faster you will grow.							
EVENTS Promote an event. Host, attend, and/or present at an event.							
3-WAY CALL ZOOM Schedule, support, connect							
PRESENTING Your story, company, product, business							

Week of ___________

If you can imagine it, you can achieve it; if you can dream it, you can become it. –William Arthur Ward
If you can imagine it, you can achieve it; if you can dream it, you can become it. –William Arthur Ward
If you can imagine it, you can achieve it; if you can dream it, you can become it. –William Arthur Ward
If you can imagine it, you can achieve it; if you can dream it, you can become it. –William Arthur Ward

Go confidently in the direction of your dreams. Live the life you have imagined. – Henry David Thoreau
Go confidently in the direction of your dreams. Live the life you have imagined. – Henry David Thoreau
Go confidently in the direction of your dreams. Live the life you have imagined. – Henry David Thoreau
Go confidently in the direction of your dreams. Live the life you have imagined. – Henry David Thoreau

Social Media ContentPlanner

Sunday	Monday	Tuesday	Wednesday	Thursday	Friday	Saturday

Week of:

Activities	MONDAY	TUESDAY	WEDNESDAY	THURSDAY	FRIDAY	SATURDAY	SUNDAY
TWO NEW PEOPLE New or memory jogger people. First time or reconnect.							
TWO NEW SHARES Share story, video, invite to group or event.							
TWO FOLLOW-UPS • Is this a good time to talk? • What did you like best about the info shared? • Are you ready to get started?							
TWO CUSTOMERS Customer Care Check-ins Add to FB group Referral Program							
SOCIAL MEDIA Post and comment (on your feed and in groups) 80/20 rule							
PERSONAL GROWTH Books, Audios, training call/zooms.							
TWO TEAM Connections and help with NEXT STEPS. Set up 3-way calls or zoom.							
Although the following may not occur daily, the more frequent they occur, the faster you will grow.							
EVENTS Promote an event. Host, attend, and/or present at an event.							
3-WAY CALL ZOOM Schedule, support, connect							
PRESENTING Your story, company, product, business							

Week of ____________

If you can imagine it, you can achieve it; if you can dream it, you can become it. —William Arthur Ward

If you can imagine it, you can achieve it; if you can dream it, you can become it. —William Arthur Ward

If you can imagine it, you can achieve it; if you can dream it, you can become it. —William Arthur Ward

If you can imagine it, you can achieve it; if you can dream it, you can become it. —William Arthur Ward

Go confidently in the direction of your dreams. Live the life you have imagined. – Henry David Thoreau

Go confidently in the direction of your dreams. Live the life you have imagined. – Henry David Thoreau

Go confidently in the direction of your dreams. Live the life you have imagined. – Henry David Thoreau

Go confidently in the direction of your dreams. Live the life you have imagined. – Henry David Thoreau

Social Media ContentPlanner

Sunday	Monday	Tuesday	Wednesday	Thursday	Friday	Saturday

Week of:

Activities	MONDAY	TUESDAY	WEDNESDAY	THURSDAY	FRIDAY	SATURDAY	SUNDAY
TWO NEW PEOPLE New or memory jogger people. First time or reconnect.							
TWO NEW SHARES Share story, video, invite to group or event.							
TWO FOLLOW-UPS • Is this a good time to talk? • What did you like best about the info shared? • Are you ready to get started?							
TWO CUSTOMERS Customer Care Check-ins Add to FB group Referral Program							
SOCIAL MEDIA Post and comment (on your feed and in groups) 80/20 rule							
PERSONAL GROWTH Books, Audios, training call/zooms.							
TWO TEAM Connections and help with NEXT STEPS. Set up 3-way calls or zoom.							
Although the following may not occur daily, the more frequent they occur, the faster you will grow.							
EVENTS Promote an event. Host, attend, and/or present at an event.							
3-WAY CALL ZOOM Schedule, support, connect							
PRESENTING Your story, company, product, business							

Week of ____________

If you can imagine it, you can achieve it; if you can dream it, you can become it. —William Arthur Ward

If you can imagine it, you can achieve it; if you can dream it, you can become it. —William Arthur Ward

If you can imagine it, you can achieve it; if you can dream it, you can become it. —William Arthur Ward

If you can imagine it, you can achieve it; if you can dream it, you can become it. —William Arthur Ward

Go confidently in the direction of your dreams. Live the life you have imagined. – Henry David Thoreau

Go confidently in the direction of your dreams. Live the life you have imagined. – Henry David Thoreau

Go confidently in the direction of your dreams. Live the life you have imagined. – Henry David Thoreau

Go confidently in the direction of your dreams. Live the life you have imagined. – Henry David Thoreau

Social Media Content Planner

Sunday	Monday	Tuesday	Wednesday	Thursday	Friday	Saturday

Week of:

Activities	MONDAY	TUESDAY	WEDNESDAY	THURSDAY	FRIDAY	SATURDAY	SUNDAY
TWO NEW PEOPLE New or memory jogger people. First time or reconnect.							
TWO NEW SHARES Share story, video, invite to group or event.							
TWO FOLLOW-UPS • Is this a good time to talk? • What did you like best about the info shared? • Are you ready to get started?							
TWO CUSTOMERS Customer Care Check-ins Add to FB group Referral Program							
SOCIAL MEDIA Post and comment (on your feed and in groups) 80/20 rule							
PERSONAL GROWTH Books, Audios, training call/zooms.							
TWO TEAM Connections and help with NEXT STEPS. Set up 3-way calls or zoom.							
Although the following may not occur daily, the more frequent they occur, the faster you will grow.							
EVENTS Promote an event. Host, attend, and/or present at an event.							
3-WAY CALL ZOOM Schedule, support, connect							
PRESENTING Your story, company, product, business							

Week of ____________

If you can imagine it, you can achieve it; if you can dream it, you can become it. —William Arthur Ward

If you can imagine it, you can achieve it; if you can dream it, you can become it. —William Arthur Ward

If you can imagine it, you can achieve it; if you can dream it, you can become it. —William Arthur Ward

If you can imagine it, you can achieve it; if you can dream it, you can become it. —William Arthur Ward

Go confidently in the direction of your dreams. Live the life you have imagined. – Henry David Thoreau

Go confidently in the direction of your dreams. Live the life you have imagined. – Henry David Thoreau

Go confidently in the direction of your dreams. Live the life you have imagined. – Henry David Thoreau

Go confidently in the direction of your dreams. Live the life you have imagined. – Henry David Thoreau

Social Media ContentPlanner

Sunday	Monday	Tuesday	Wednesday	Thursday	Friday	Saturday

Week of:

Activities	MONDAY	TUESDAY	WEDNESDAY	THURSDAY	FRIDAY	SATURDAY	SUNDAY
TWO NEW PEOPLE New or memory jogger people. First time or reconnect.							
TWO NEW SHARES Share story, video, invite to group or event.							
TWO FOLLOW-UPS • Is this a good time to talk? • What did you like best about the info shared? • Are you ready to get started?							
TWO CUSTOMERS Customer Care Check-ins Add to FB group Referral Program							
SOCIAL MEDIA Post and comment (on your feed and in groups) 80/20 rule							
PERSONAL GROWTH Books, Audios, training call/zooms.							
TWO TEAM Connections and help with NEXT STEPS. Set up 3-way calls or zoom.							
Although the following may not occur daily, the more frequent they occur, the faster you will grow.							
EVENTS Promote an event. Host, attend, and/or present at an event.							
3-WAY CALL ZOOM Schedule, support, connect							
PRESENTING Your story, company, product, business							

Week of ______________

If you can imagine it, you can achieve it; if you can dream it, you can become it. –William Arthur Ward

If you can imagine it, you can achieve it; if you can dream it, you can become it. –William Arthur Ward

If you can imagine it, you can achieve it; if you can dream it, you can become it. –William Arthur Ward

If you can imagine it, you can achieve it; if you can dream it, you can become it. –William Arthur Ward

Go confidently in the direction of your dreams. Live the life you have imagined. – Henry David Thoreau

Go confidently in the direction of your dreams. Live the life you have imagined. – Henry David Thoreau

Go confidently in the direction of your dreams. Live the life you have imagined. – Henry David Thoreau

Go confidently in the direction of your dreams. Live the life you have imagined. – Henry David Thoreau

Social Media ContentPlanner

Sunday	Monday	Tuesday	Wednesday	Thursday	Friday	Saturday

Week of:

Activities	MONDAY	TUESDAY	WEDNESDAY	THURSDAY	FRIDAY	SATURDAY	SUNDAY
TWO NEW PEOPLE New or memory jogger people. First time or reconnect.							
TWO NEW SHARES Share story, video, invite to group or event.							
TWO FOLLOW-UPS • Is this a good time to talk? • What did you like best about the info shared? • Are you ready to get started?							
TWO CUSTOMERS Customer Care Check-ins Add to FB group Referral Program							
SOCIAL MEDIA Post and comment (on your feed and in groups) 80/20 rule							
PERSONAL GROWTH Books, Audios, training call/zooms.							
TWO TEAM Connections and help with NEXT STEPS. Set up 3-way calls or zoom.							
Although the following may not occur daily, the more frequent they occur, the faster you will grow.							
EVENTS Promote an event. Host, attend, and/or present at an event.							
3-WAY CALL ZOOM Schedule, support, connect							
PRESENTING Your story, company, product, business							

Week of ____________

If you can imagine it, you can achieve it. If you can dream it, you can become it. –William Arthur Ward
If you can imagine it, you can achieve it. If you can dream it, you can become it. –William Arthur Ward
If you can imagine it, you can achieve it. If you can dream it, you can become it. –William Arthur Ward
If you can imagine it, you can achieve it. If you can dream it, you can become it. –William Arthur Ward

Go confidently in the direction of your dreams. Live the life you have imagined. – Henry David Thoreau
Go confidently in the direction of your dreams. Live the life you have imagined. – Henry David Thoreau
Go confidently in the direction of your dreams. Live the life you have imagined. – Henry David Thoreau
Go confidently in the direction of your dreams. Live the life you have imagined. – Henry David Thoreau

Social Media ContentPlanner

Sunday	Monday	Tuesday	Wednesday	Thursday	Friday	Saturday

Week of:

Activities	MONDAY	TUESDAY	WEDNESDAY	THURSDAY	FRIDAY	SATURDAY	SUNDAY
TWO NEW PEOPLE New or memory jogger people. First time or reconnect.							
TWO NEW SHARES Share story, video, invite to group or event.							
TWO FOLLOW-UPS • Is this a good time to talk? • What did you like best about the info shared? • Are you ready to get started?							
TWO CUSTOMERS Customer Care Check-ins Add to FB group Referral Program							
SOCIAL MEDIA Post and comment (on your feed and in groups) 80/20 rule							
PERSONAL GROWTH Books, Audios, training call/zooms.							
TWO TEAM Connections and help with NEXT STEPS. Set up 3-way calls or zoom.							
Although the following may not occur daily, the more frequent they occur, the faster you will grow.							
EVENTS Promote an event. Host, attend, and/or present at an event.							
3-WAY CALL ZOOM Schedule, support, connect							
PRESENTING Your story, company, product, business							

Week of ______________

If you can imagine it, you can achieve it; if you can dream it, you can become it. –William Arthur Ward

If you can imagine it, you can achieve it; if you can dream it, you can become it. –William Arthur Ward
If you can imagine it, you can achieve it; if you can dream it, you can become it. –William Arthur Ward
If you can imagine it, you can achieve it; if you can dream it, you can become it. –William Arthur Ward

Go confidently in the direction of your dreams. Live the life you have imagined. – Henry David Thoreau

Go confidently in the direction of your dreams. Live the life you have imagined. – Henry David Thoreau
Go confidently in the direction of your dreams. Live the life you have imagined. – Henry David Thoreau
Go confidently in the direction of your dreams. Live the life you have imagined. – Henry David Thoreau

Social Media Content Planner

Sunday	Monday	Tuesday	Wednesday	Thursday	Friday	Saturday

Week of:

Activities	MONDAY	TUESDAY	WEDNESDAY	THURSDAY	FRIDAY	SATURDAY	SUNDAY
TWO NEW PEOPLE New or memory jogger people. First time or reconnect.							
TWO NEW SHARES Share story, video, invite to group or event.							
TWO FOLLOW-UPS • Is this a good time to talk? • What did you like best about the info shared? • Are you ready to get started?							
TWO CUSTOMERS Customer Care Check-ins Add to FB group Referral Program							
SOCIAL MEDIA Post and comment (on your feed and in groups) 80/20 rule							
PERSONAL GROWTH Books, Audios, training call/zooms.							
TWO TEAM Connections and help with NEXT STEPS. Set up 3-way calls or zoom.							
Although the following may not occur daily, the more frequent they occur, the faster you will grow.							
EVENTS Promote an event. Host, attend, and/or present at an event.							
3-WAY CALL ZOOM Schedule, support, connect							
PRESENTING Your story, company, product, business							

Week of ______________

If you can imagine it, you can achieve it; if you can dream it, you can become it. –William Arthur Ward

If you can imagine it, you can achieve it; if you can dream it, you can become it. –William Arthur Ward

If you can imagine it, you can achieve it; if you can dream it, you can become it. –William Arthur Ward

If you can imagine it, you can achieve it; if you can dream it, you can become it. –William Arthur Ward

Go confidently in the direction of your dreams. Live the life you have imagined. – Henry David Thoreau

Go confidently in the direction of your dreams. Live the life you have imagined. – Henry David Thoreau

Go confidently in the direction of your dreams. Live the life you have imagined. – Henry David Thoreau

Go confidently in the direction of your dreams. Live the life you have imagined. – Henry David Thoreau

Social Media ContentPlanner

Sunday	Monday	Tuesday	Wednesday	Thursday	Friday	Saturday

Week of:

Activities	MONDAY	TUESDAY	WEDNESDAY	THURSDAY	FRIDAY	SATURDAY	SUNDAY
TWO NEW PEOPLE New or memory jogger people. First time or reconnect.							
TWO NEW SHARES Share story, video, invite to group or event.							
TWO FOLLOW-UPS • Is this a good time to talk? • What did you like best about the info shared? • Are you ready to get started?							
TWO CUSTOMERS Customer Care Check-ins Add to FB group Referral Program							
SOCIAL MEDIA Post and comment (on your feed and in groups) 80/20 rule							
PERSONAL GROWTH Books, Audios, training call/zooms.							
TWO TEAM Connections and help with NEXT STEPS. Set up 3-way calls or zoom.							
Although the following may not occur daily, the more frequent they occur, the faster you will grow.							
EVENTS Promote an event. Host, attend, and/or present at an event.							
3-WAY CALL ZOOM Schedule, support, connect							
PRESENTING Your story, company, product, business							

Week of ______________

If you can imagine it, you can achieve it; if you can dream it, you can become it. –William Arthur Ward

If you can imagine it, you can achieve it; if you can dream it, you can become it. –William Arthur Ward

If you can imagine it, you can achieve it; if you can dream it, you can become it. –William Arthur Ward

If you can imagine it, you can achieve it; if you can dream it, you can become it. –William Arthur Ward

Go confidently in the direction of your dreams. Live the life you have imagined. – Henry David Thoreau

Go confidently in the direction of your dreams. Live the life you have imagined. – Henry David Thoreau

Go confidently in the direction of your dreams. Live the life you have imagined. – Henry David Thoreau

Go confidently in the direction of your dreams. Live the life you have imagined. – Henry David Thoreau

Social Media ContentPlanner

Sunday	Monday	Tuesday	Wednesday	Thursday	Friday	Saturday

Week of:

Activities	MONDAY	TUESDAY	WEDNESDAY	THURSDAY	FRIDAY	SATURDAY	SUNDAY
TWO NEW PEOPLE New or memory jogger people. First time or reconnect.							
TWO NEW SHARES Share story, video, invite to group or event.							
TWO FOLLOW-UPS • Is this a good time to talk? • What did you like best about the info shared? • Are you ready to get started?							
TWO CUSTOMERS Customer Care Check-ins Add to FB group Referral Program							
SOCIAL MEDIA Post and comment (on your feed and in groups) 80/20 rule							
PERSONAL GROWTH Books, Audios, training call/zooms.							
TWO TEAM Connections and help with NEXT STEPS. Set up 3-way calls or zoom.							
Although the following may not occur daily, the more frequent they occur, the faster you will grow.							
EVENTS Promote an event. Host, attend, and/or present at an event.							
3-WAY CALL ZOOM Schedule, support, connect							
PRESENTING Your story, company, product, business							

Week of ______________

If you can imagine it, you can achieve it; if you can dream it, you can become it. – William Arthur Ward

If you can imagine it, you can achieve it; if you can dream it, you can become it. – William Arthur Ward

If you can imagine it, you can achieve it; if you can dream it, you can become it. – William Arthur Ward

If you can imagine it, you can achieve it; if you can dream it, you can become it. – William Arthur Ward

Go confidently in the direction of your dreams. Live the life you have imagined. – Henry David Thoreau

Go confidently in the direction of your dreams. Live the life you have imagined. – Henry David Thoreau

Go confidently in the direction of your dreams. Live the life you have imagined. – Henry David Thoreau

Go confidently in the direction of your dreams. Live the life you have imagined. – Henry David Thoreau

Social Media ContentPlanner

Sunday	Monday	Tuesday	Wednesday	Thursday	Friday	Saturday

Week of:

Activities	MONDAY	TUESDAY	WEDNESDAY	THURSDAY	FRIDAY	SATURDAY	SUNDAY
TWO NEW PEOPLE New or memory jogger people. First time or reconnect.							
TWO NEW SHARES Share story, video, invite to group or event.							
TWO FOLLOW-UPS • Is this a good time to talk? • What did you like best about the info shared? • Are you ready to get started?							
TWO CUSTOMERS Customer Care Check-ins Add to FB group Referral Program							
SOCIAL MEDIA Post and comment (on your feed and in groups) 80/20 rule							
PERSONAL GROWTH Books, Audios, training call/zooms.							
TWO TEAM Connections and help with NEXT STEPS. Set up 3-way calls or zoom.							
Although the following may not occur daily, the more frequent they occur, the faster you will grow.							
EVENTS Promote an event. Host, attend, and/or present at an event.							
3-WAY CALL ZOOM Schedule, support, connect							
PRESENTING Your story, company, product, business							

Week of ______________

If you can imagine it, you can achieve it; if you can dream it, you can become it. –William Arthur Ward

If you can imagine it, you can achieve it; if you can dream it, you can become it. –William Arthur Ward

If you can imagine it, you can achieve it; if you can dream it, you can become it. –William Arthur Ward

If you can imagine it, you can achieve it; if you can dream it, you can become it. –William Arthur Ward

Go confidently in the direction of your dreams. Live the life you have imagined. – Henry David Thoreau

Go confidently in the direction of your dreams. Live the life you have imagined. – Henry David Thoreau

Go confidently in the direction of your dreams. Live the life you have imagined. – Henry David Thoreau

Go confidently in the direction of your dreams. Live the life you have imagined. – Henry David Thoreau

Social Media ContentPlanner

Sunday	Monday	Tuesday	Wednesday	Thursday	Friday	Saturday

Week of:

Activities	MONDAY	TUESDAY	WEDNESDAY	THURSDAY	FRIDAY	SATURDAY	SUNDAY
TWO NEW PEOPLE New or memory jogger people. First time or reconnect.							
TWO NEW SHARES Share story, video, invite to group or event.							
TWO FOLLOW-UPS • Is this a good time to talk? • What did you like best about the info shared? • Are you ready to get started?							
TWO CUSTOMERS Customer Care Check-ins Add to FB group Referral Program							
SOCIAL MEDIA Post and comment (on your feed and in groups) 80/20 rule							
PERSONAL GROWTH Books, Audios, training call/zooms.							
TWO TEAM Connections and help with NEXT STEPS. Set up 3-way calls or zoom.							
Although the following may not occur daily, the more frequent they occur, the faster you will grow.							
EVENTS Promote an event. Host, attend, and/or present at an event.							
3-WAY CALL ZOOM Schedule, support, connect							
PRESENTING Your story, company, product, business							

Week of ____________

If you can imagine it, you can achieve it, if you can dream it, you can become it. —William Arthur Ward
If you can imagine it, you can achieve it, if you can dream it, you can become it. —William Arthur Ward
If you can imagine it, you can achieve it, if you can dream it, you can become it. —William Arthur Ward
If you can imagine it, you can achieve it, if you can dream it, you can become it. —William Arthur Ward

Go confidently in the direction of your dreams. Live the life you have imagined. – Henry David Thoreau
Go confidently in the direction of your dreams. Live the life you have imagined. – Henry David Thoreau
Go confidently in the direction of your dreams. Live the life you have imagined. – Henry David Thoreau
Go confidently in the direction of your dreams. Live the life you have imagined. – Henry David Thoreau

Social Media ContentPlanner

Sunday	Monday	Tuesday	Wednesday	Thursday	Friday	Saturday

Week of:

Activities	MONDAY	TUESDAY	WEDNESDAY	THURSDAY	FRIDAY	SATURDAY	SUNDAY
TWO NEW PEOPLE New or memory jogger people. First time or reconnect.							
TWO NEW SHARES Share story, video, invite to group or event.							
TWO FOLLOW-UPS • Is this a good time to talk? • What did you like best about the info shared? • Are you ready to get started?							
TWO CUSTOMERS Customer Care Check-ins Add to FB group Referral Program							
SOCIAL MEDIA Post and comment (on your feed and in groups) 80/20 rule							
PERSONAL GROWTH Books, Audios, training call/zooms.							
TWO TEAM Connections and help with NEXT STEPS. Set up 3-way calls or zoom.							
Although the following may not occur daily, the more frequent they occur, the faster you will grow.							
EVENTS Promote an event. Host, attend, and/or present at an event.							
3-WAY CALL ZOOM Schedule, support, connect							
PRESENTING Your story, company, product, business							

Week of ____________

If you can imagine it, you can achieve it; if you can dream it, you can become it. –William Arthur Ward

If you can imagine it, you can achieve it; if you can dream it, you can become it. –William Arthur Ward

If you can imagine it, you can achieve it; if you can dream it, you can become it. –William Arthur Ward

If you can imagine it, you can achieve it; if you can dream it, you can become it. –William Arthur Ward

Go confidently in the direction of your dreams. Live the life you have imagined. – Henry David Thoreau

Go confidently in the direction of your dreams. Live the life you have imagined. – Henry David Thoreau

Go confidently in the direction of your dreams. Live the life you have imagined. – Henry David Thoreau

Go confidently in the direction of your dreams. Live the life you have imagined. – Henry David Thoreau

Social Media ContentPlanner

Sunday	Monday	Tuesday	Wednesday	Thursday	Friday	Saturday

Week of:

Activities	MONDAY	TUESDAY	WEDNESDAY	THURSDAY	FRIDAY	SATURDAY	SUNDAY
TWO NEW PEOPLE New or memory jogger people. First time or reconnect.							
TWO NEW SHARES Share story, video, invite to group or event.							
TWO FOLLOW-UPS • Is this a good time to talk? • What did you like best about the info shared? • Are you ready to get started?							
TWO CUSTOMERS Customer Care Check-ins Add to FB group Referral Program							
SOCIAL MEDIA Post and comment (on your feed and in groups) 80/20 rule							
PERSONAL GROWTH Books, Audios, training call/zooms.							
TWO TEAM Connections and help with NEXT STEPS. Set up 3-way calls or zoom.							
Although the following may not occur daily, the more frequent they occur, the faster you will grow.							
EVENTS Promote an event. Host, attend, and/or present at an event.							
3-WAY CALL ZOOM Schedule, support, connect							
PRESENTING Your story, company, product, business							

Week of ____________

If you can imagine it, you can achieve it; if you can dream it, you can become it. – William Arthur Ward

If you can imagine it, you can achieve it; if you can dream it, you can become it. – William Arthur Ward

If you can imagine it, you can achieve it; if you can dream it, you can become it. – William Arthur Ward

If you can imagine it, you can achieve it; if you can dream it, you can become it. – William Arthur Ward

Go confidently in the direction of your dreams. Live the life you have imagined. – Henry David Thoreau

Go confidently in the direction of your dreams. Live the life you have imagined. – Henry David Thoreau

Go confidently in the direction of your dreams. Live the life you have imagined. – Henry David Thoreau

Go confidently in the direction of your dreams. Live the life you have imagined. – Henry David Thoreau

Social Media ContentPlanner

Sunday	Monday	Tuesday	Wednesday	Thursday	Friday	Saturday

Week of:

Activities	MONDAY	TUESDAY	WEDNESDAY	THURSDAY	FRIDAY	SATURDAY	SUNDAY
TWO NEW PEOPLE New or memory jogger people. First time or reconnect.							
TWO NEW SHARES Share story, video, invite to group or event.							
TWO FOLLOW-UPS • Is this a good time to talk? • What did you like best about the info shared? • Are you ready to get started?							
TWO CUSTOMERS Customer Care Check-ins Add to FB group Referral Program							
SOCIAL MEDIA Post and comment (on your feed and in groups) 80/20 rule							
PERSONAL GROWTH Books, Audios, training call/zooms.							
TWO TEAM Connections and help with NEXT STEPS. Set up 3-way calls or zoom.							
Although the following may not occur daily, the more frequent they occur, the faster you will grow.							
EVENTS Promote an event. Host, attend, and/or present at an event.							
3-WAY CALL ZOOM Schedule, support, connect							
PRESENTING Your story, company, product, business							

Week of ______________

If you can imagine it, you can achieve it; if you can dream it, you can become it. —William Arthur Ward

If you can imagine it, you can achieve it; if you can dream it, you can become it. —William Arthur Ward

If you can imagine it, you can achieve it; if you can dream it, you can become it. —William Arthur Ward

If you can imagine it, you can achieve it; if you can dream it, you can become it. —William Arthur Ward

Go confidently in the direction of your dreams. Live the life you have imagined. – Henry David Thoreau

Go confidently in the direction of your dreams. Live the life you have imagined. – Henry David Thoreau

Go confidently in the direction of your dreams. Live the life you have imagined. – Henry David Thoreau

Go confidently in the direction of your dreams. Live the life you have imagined. – Henry David Thoreau

Social Media ContentPlanner

Sunday	Monday	Tuesday	Wednesday	Thursday	Friday	Saturday

Week of:

Activities	MONDAY	TUESDAY	WEDNESDAY	THURSDAY	FRIDAY	SATURDAY	SUNDAY
TWO NEW PEOPLE New or memory jogger people. First time or reconnect.							
TWO NEW SHARES Share story, video, invite to group or event.							
TWO FOLLOW-UPS • Is this a good time to talk? • What did you like best about the info shared? • Are you ready to get started?							
TWO CUSTOMERS Customer Care Check-ins Add to FB group Referral Program							
SOCIAL MEDIA Post and comment (on your feed and in groups) 80/20 rule							
PERSONAL GROWTH Books, Audios, training call/zooms.							
TWO TEAM Connections and help with NEXT STEPS. Set up 3-way calls or zoom.							
Although the following may not occur daily, the more frequent they occur, the faster you will grow.							
EVENTS Promote an event. Host, attend, and/or present at an event.							
3-WAY CALL ZOOM Schedule, support, connect							
PRESENTING Your story, company, product, business							

Week of ______________

If you can imagine it, you can achieve it; if you can dream it, you can become it. –William Arthur Ward

If you can imagine it, you can achieve it; if you can dream it, you can become it. –William Arthur Ward

If you can imagine it, you can achieve it; if you can dream it, you can become it. –William Arthur Ward

If you can imagine it, you can achieve it; if you can dream it, you can become it. –William Arthur Ward

Go confidently in the direction of your dreams. Live the life you have imagined. – Henry David Thoreau

Go confidently in the direction of your dreams. Live the life you have imagined. – Henry David Thoreau

Go confidently in the direction of your dreams. Live the life you have imagined. – Henry David Thoreau

Go confidently in the direction of your dreams. Live the life you have imagined. – Henry David Thoreau

Social Media ContentPlanner

Sunday	Monday	Tuesday	Wednesday	Thursday	Friday	Saturday

Week of:

Activities	MONDAY	TUESDAY	WEDNESDAY	THURSDAY	FRIDAY	SATURDAY	SUNDAY
TWO NEW PEOPLE New or memory jogger people. First time or reconnect.							
TWO NEW SHARES Share story, video, invite to group or event.							
TWO FOLLOW-UPS • Is this a good time to talk? • What did you like best about the info shared? • Are you ready to get started?							
TWO CUSTOMERS Customer Care Check-ins Add to FB group Referral Program							
SOCIAL MEDIA Post and comment (on your feed and in groups) 80/20 rule							
PERSONAL GROWTH Books, Audios, training call/zooms.							
TWO TEAM Connections and help with NEXT STEPS. Set up 3-way calls or zoom.							
Although the following may not occur daily, the more frequent they occur, the faster you will grow.							
EVENTS Promote an event. Host, attend, and/or present at an event.							
3-WAY CALL ZOOM Schedule, support, connect							
PRESENTING Your story, company, product, business							

Week of ____________

If you can imagine it, you can achieve it; if you can dream it, you can become it. —William Arthur Ward

If you can imagine it, you can achieve it; if you can dream it, you can become it. —William Arthur Ward
If you can imagine it, you can achieve it; if you can dream it, you can become it. —William Arthur Ward
If you can imagine it, you can achieve it; if you can dream it, you can become it. —William Arthur Ward

Go confidently in the direction of your dreams. Live the life you have imagined. – Henry David Thoreau

Go confidently in the direction of your dreams. Live the life you have imagined. – Henry David Thoreau
Go confidently in the direction of your dreams. Live the life you have imagined. – Henry David Thoreau
Go confidently in the direction of your dreams. Live the life you have imagined. – Henry David Thoreau

Social Media ContentPlanner

Sunday	Monday	Tuesday	Wednesday	Thursday	Friday	Saturday

Week of:

Activities	MONDAY	TUESDAY	WEDNESDAY	THURSDAY	FRIDAY	SATURDAY	SUNDAY
TWO NEW PEOPLE New or memory jogger people. First time or reconnect.							
TWO NEW SHARES Share story, video, invite to group or event.							
TWO FOLLOW-UPS • Is this a good time to talk? • What did you like best about the info shared? • Are you ready to get started?							
TWO CUSTOMERS Customer Care Check-ins Add to FB group Referral Program							
SOCIAL MEDIA Post and comment (on your feed and in groups) 80/20 rule							
PERSONAL GROWTH Books, Audios, training call/zooms.							
TWO TEAM Connections and help with NEXT STEPS. Set up 3-way calls or zoom.							
Although the following may not occur daily, the more frequent they occur, the faster you will grow.							
EVENTS Promote an event. Host, attend, and/or present at an event.							
3-WAY CALL ZOOM Schedule, support, connect							
PRESENTING Your story, company, product, business							

Week of ______________

If you can imagine it, you can achieve it; if you can dream it, you can become it. –William Arthur Ward

If you can imagine it, you can achieve it; if you can dream it, you can become it. –William Arthur Ward

If you can imagine it, you can achieve it; if you can dream it, you can become it. –William Arthur Ward

If you can imagine it, you can achieve it; if you can dream it, you can become it. –William Arthur Ward

Go confidently in the direction of your dreams. Live the life you have imagined. – Henry David Thoreau

Go confidently in the direction of your dreams. Live the life you have imagined. – Henry David Thoreau

Go confidently in the direction of your dreams. Live the life you have imagined. – Henry David Thoreau

Go confidently in the direction of your dreams. Live the life you have imagined. – Henry David Thoreau

Social Media ContentPlanner

Sunday	Monday	Tuesday	Wednesday	Thursday	Friday	Saturday

Week of:

Activities	MONDAY	TUESDAY	WEDNESDAY	THURSDAY	FRIDAY	SATURDAY	SUNDAY
TWO NEW PEOPLE New or memory jogger people. First time or reconnect.							
TWO NEW SHARES Share story, video, invite to group or event.							
TWO FOLLOW-UPS • Is this a good time to talk? • What did you like best about the info shared? • Are you ready to get started?							
TWO CUSTOMERS Customer Care Check-ins Add to FB group Referral Program							
SOCIAL MEDIA Post and comment (on your feed and in groups) 80/20 rule							
PERSONAL GROWTH Books, Audios, training call/zooms.							
TWO TEAM Connections and help with NEXT STEPS. Set up 3-way calls or zoom.							
Although the following may not occur daily, the more frequent they occur, the faster you will grow.							
EVENTS Promote an event. Host, attend, and/or present at an event.							
3-WAY CALL ZOOM Schedule, support, connect							
PRESENTING Your story, company, product, business							

Week of ____________

If you can imagine it, you can achieve it; if you can dream it, you can become it. – William Arthur Ward

If you can imagine it, you can achieve it; if you can dream it, you can become it. – William Arthur Ward
If you can imagine it, you can achieve it; if you can dream it, you can become it. – William Arthur Ward
If you can imagine it, you can achieve it; if you can dream it, you can become it. – William Arthur Ward

Go confidently in the direction of your dreams. Live the life you have imagined. – Henry David Thoreau

Go confidently in the direction of your dreams. Live the life you have imagined. – Henry David Thoreau
Go confidently in the direction of your dreams. Live the life you have imagined. – Henry David Thoreau
Go confidently in the direction of your dreams. Live the life you have imagined. – Henry David Thoreau

Social Media ContentPlanner

Sunday	Monday	Tuesday	Wednesday	Thursday	Friday	Saturday

Week of:

Activities	MONDAY	TUESDAY	WEDNESDAY	THURSDAY	FRIDAY	SATURDAY	SUNDAY
TWO NEW PEOPLE New or memory jogger people. First time or reconnect.							
TWO NEW SHARES Share story, video, invite to group or event.							
TWO FOLLOW-UPS • Is this a good time to talk? • What did you like best about the info shared? • Are you ready to get started?							
TWO CUSTOMERS Customer Care Check-ins Add to FB group Referral Program							
SOCIAL MEDIA Post and comment (on your feed and in groups) 80/20 rule							
PERSONAL GROWTH Books, Audios, training call/zooms.							
TWO TEAM Connections and help with NEXT STEPS. Set up 3-way calls or zoom.							
Although the following may not occur daily, the more frequent they occur, the faster you will grow.							
EVENTS Promote an event. Host, attend, and/or present at an event.							
3-WAY CALL ZOOM Schedule, support, connect							
PRESENTING Your story, company, product, business							

Week of ___________

If you can imagine it, you can achieve it; if you can dream it, you can become it. —William Arthur Ward

If you can imagine it, you can achieve it; if you can dream it, you can become it. —William Arthur Ward

If you can imagine it, you can achieve it; if you can dream it, you can become it. —William Arthur Ward

If you can imagine it, you can achieve it; if you can dream it, you can become it. —William Arthur Ward

Go confidently in the direction of your dreams. Live the life you have imagined. – Henry David Thoreau

Go confidently in the direction of your dreams. Live the life you have imagined. – Henry David Thoreau

Go confidently in the direction of your dreams. Live the life you have imagined. – Henry David Thoreau

Go confidently in the direction of your dreams. Live the life you have imagined. – Henry David Thoreau

Social Media ContentPlanner

Sunday	Monday	Tuesday	Wednesday	Thursday	Friday	Saturday

Week of:

Activities	MONDAY	TUESDAY	WEDNESDAY	THURSDAY	FRIDAY	SATURDAY	SUNDAY
TWO NEW PEOPLE New or memory jogger people. First time or reconnect.							
TWO NEW SHARES Share story, video, invite to group or event.							
TWO FOLLOW-UPS • Is this a good time to talk? • What did you like best about the info shared? • Are you ready to get started?							
TWO CUSTOMERS Customer Care Check-ins Add to FB group Referral Program							
SOCIAL MEDIA Post and comment (on your feed and in groups) 80/20 rule							
PERSONAL GROWTH Books, Audios, training call/zooms.							
TWO TEAM Connections and help with NEXT STEPS. Set up 3-way calls or zoom.							
Although the following may not occur daily, the more frequent they occur, the faster you will grow.							
EVENTS Promote an event. Host, attend, and/or present at an event.							
3-WAY CALL ZOOM Schedule, support, connect							
PRESENTING Your story, company, product, business							

Week of ______________

If you can imagine it, you can achieve it; if you can dream it, you can become it. –William Arthur Ward

If you can imagine it, you can achieve it; if you can dream it, you can become it. –William Arthur Ward

If you can imagine it, you can achieve it; if you can dream it, you can become it. –William Arthur Ward

If you can imagine it, you can achieve it; if you can dream it, you can become it. –William Arthur Ward

Go confidently in the direction of your dreams. Live the life you have imagined. – Henry David Thoreau

Go confidently in the direction of your dreams. Live the life you have imagined. – Henry David Thoreau

Go confidently in the direction of your dreams. Live the life you have imagined. – Henry David Thoreau

Go confidently in the direction of your dreams. Live the life you have imagined. – Henry David Thoreau

Social Media ContentPlanner

Sunday	Monday	Tuesday	Wednesday	Thursday	Friday	Saturday

Week of:

Activities	MONDAY	TUESDAY	WEDNESDAY	THURSDAY	FRIDAY	SATURDAY	SUNDAY
TWO NEW PEOPLE New or memory jogger people. First time or reconnect.							
TWO NEW SHARES Share story, video, invite to group or event.							
TWO FOLLOW-UPS • Is this a good time to talk? • What did you like best about the info shared? • Are you ready to get started?							
TWO CUSTOMERS Customer Care Check-ins Add to FB group Referral Program							
SOCIAL MEDIA Post and comment (on your feed and in groups) 80/20 rule							
PERSONAL GROWTH Books, Audios, training call/zooms.							
TWO TEAM Connections and help with NEXT STEPS. Set up 3-way calls or zoom.							
Although the following may not occur daily, the more frequent they occur, the faster you will grow.							
EVENTS Promote an event. Host, attend, and/or present at an event.							
3-WAY CALL ZOOM Schedule, support, connect							
PRESENTING Your story, company, product, business							

Week of ______________

If you can imagine it, you can achieve it; if you can dream it, you can become it. —William Arthur Ward

If you can imagine it, you can achieve it; if you can dream it, you can become it. —William Arthur Ward

If you can imagine it, you can achieve it; if you can dream it, you can become it. —William Arthur Ward

If you can imagine it, you can achieve it; if you can dream it, you can become it. —William Arthur Ward

Go confidently in the direction of your dreams. Live the life you have imagined. – Henry David Thoreau

Go confidently in the direction of your dreams. Live the life you have imagined. – Henry David Thoreau

Go confidently in the direction of your dreams. Live the life you have imagined. – Henry David Thoreau

Go confidently in the direction of your dreams. Live the life you have imagined. – Henry David Thoreau

Social Media ContentPlanner

Sunday	Monday	Tuesday	Wednesday	Thursday	Friday	Saturday

Week of:

Activities	MONDAY	TUESDAY	WEDNESDAY	THURSDAY	FRIDAY	SATURDAY	SUNDAY
TWO NEW PEOPLE New or memory jogger people. First time or reconnect.							
TWO NEW SHARES Share story, video, invite to group or event.							
TWO FOLLOW-UPS • Is this a good time to talk? • What did you like best about the info shared? • Are you ready to get started?							
TWO CUSTOMERS Customer Care Check-ins Add to FB group Referral Program							
SOCIAL MEDIA Post and comment (on your feed and in groups) 80/20 rule							
PERSONAL GROWTH Books, Audios, training call/zooms.							
TWO TEAM Connections and help with NEXT STEPS. Set up 3-way calls or zoom.							
Although the following may not occur daily, the more frequent they occur, the faster you will grow.							
EVENTS Promote an event. Host, attend, and/or present at an event.							
3-WAY CALL ZOOM Schedule, support, connect							
PRESENTING Your story, company, product, business							

Week of ____________

If you can imagine it, you can achieve it; if you can dream it, you can become it. —William Arthur Ward

If you can imagine it, you can achieve it; if you can dream it, you can become it. —William Arthur Ward

If you can imagine it, you can achieve it; if you can dream it, you can become it. —William Arthur Ward

If you can imagine it, you can achieve it; if you can dream it, you can become it. —William Arthur Ward

Go confidently in the direction of your dreams. Live the life you have imagined. – Henry David Thoreau

Go confidently in the direction of your dreams. Live the life you have imagined. – Henry David Thoreau

Go confidently in the direction of your dreams. Live the life you have imagined. – Henry David Thoreau

Go confidently in the direction of your dreams. Live the life you have imagined. – Henry David Thoreau

Social Media ContentPlanner

Sunday	Monday	Tuesday	Wednesday	Thursday	Friday	Saturday

Week of:

Activities	MONDAY	TUESDAY	WEDNESDAY	THURSDAY	FRIDAY	SATURDAY	SUNDAY
TWO NEW PEOPLE New or memory jogger people. First time or reconnect.							
TWO NEW SHARES Share story, video, invite to group or event.							
TWO FOLLOW-UPS • Is this a good time to talk? • What did you like best about the info shared? • Are you ready to get started?							
TWO CUSTOMERS Customer Care Check-ins Add to FB group Referral Program							
SOCIAL MEDIA Post and comment (on your feed and in groups) 80/20 rule							
PERSONAL GROWTH Books, Audios, training call/zooms.							
TWO TEAM Connections and help with NEXT STEPS. Set up 3-way calls or zoom.							
Although the following may not occur daily, the more frequent they occur, the faster you will grow.							
EVENTS Promote an event. Host, attend, and/or present at an event.							
3-WAY CALL ZOOM Schedule, support, connect							
PRESENTING Your story, company, product, business							

Week of ______________

If you can imagine it, you can achieve it; if you can dream it, you can become it. –William Arthur Ward

If you can imagine it, you can achieve it; if you can dream it, you can become it. –William Arthur Ward
If you can imagine it, you can achieve it; if you can dream it, you can become it. –William Arthur Ward
If you can imagine it, you can achieve it; if you can dream it, you can become it. –William Arthur Ward

Go confidently in the direction of your dreams. Live the life you have imagined. – Henry David Thoreau

Go confidently in the direction of your dreams. Live the life you have imagined. – Henry David Thoreau
Go confidently in the direction of your dreams. Live the life you have imagined. – Henry David Thoreau
Go confidently in the direction of your dreams. Live the life you have imagined. – Henry David Thoreau

Social Media Content Planner

Sunday	Monday	Tuesday	Wednesday	Thursday	Friday	Saturday

Week of:

Activities	MONDAY	TUESDAY	WEDNESDAY	THURSDAY	FRIDAY	SATURDAY	SUNDAY
TWO NEW PEOPLE New or memory jogger people. First time or reconnect.							
TWO NEW SHARES Share story, video, invite to group or event.							
TWO FOLLOW-UPS • Is this a good time to talk? • What did you like best about the info shared? • Are you ready to get started?							
TWO CUSTOMERS Customer Care Check-ins Add to FB group Referral Program							
SOCIAL MEDIA Post and comment (on your feed and in groups) 80/20 rule							
PERSONAL GROWTH Books, Audios, training call/zooms.							
TWO TEAM Connections and help with NEXT STEPS. Set up 3-way calls or zoom.							
Although the following may not occur daily, the more frequent they occur, the faster you will grow.							
EVENTS Promote an event. Host, attend, and/or present at an event.							
3-WAY CALL ZOOM Schedule, support, connect							
PRESENTING Your story, company, product, business							

Week of ____________

If you can imagine it, you can achieve it; if you can dream it, you can become it. —William Arthur Ward
If you can imagine it, you can achieve it; if you can dream it, you can become it. —William Arthur Ward
If you can imagine it, you can achieve it; if you can dream it, you can become it. —William Arthur Ward
If you can imagine it, you can achieve it; if you can dream it, you can become it. —William Arthur Ward

Go confidently in the direction of your dreams. Live the life you have imagined. – Henry David Thoreau
Go confidently in the direction of your dreams. Live the life you have imagined. – Henry David Thoreau
Go confidently in the direction of your dreams. Live the life you have imagined. – Henry David Thoreau
Go confidently in the direction of your dreams. Live the life you have imagined. – Henry David Thoreau

Social Media Content Planner

Sunday	Monday	Tuesday	Wednesday	Thursday	Friday	Saturday

Week of:

Activities	MONDAY	TUESDAY	WEDNESDAY	THURSDAY	FRIDAY	SATURDAY	SUNDAY
TWO NEW PEOPLE New or memory jogger people. First time or reconnect.							
TWO NEW SHARES Share story, video, invite to group or event.							
TWO FOLLOW-UPS • Is this a good time to talk? • What did you like best about the info shared? • Are you ready to get started?							
TWO CUSTOMERS Customer Care Check-ins Add to FB group Referral Program							
SOCIAL MEDIA Post and comment (on your feed and in groups) 80/20 rule							
PERSONAL GROWTH Books, Audios, training call/zooms.							
TWO TEAM Connections and help with NEXT STEPS. Set up 3-way calls or zoom.							
Although the following may not occur daily, the more frequent they occur, the faster you will grow.							
EVENTS Promote an event. Host, attend, and/or present at an event.							
3-WAY CALL ZOOM Schedule, support, connect							
PRESENTING Your story, company, product, business							

Week of ____________

If you can imagine it, you can achieve it; if you can dream it, you can become it. –William Arthur Ward

If you can imagine it, you can achieve it; if you can dream it, you can become it. –William Arthur Ward

If you can imagine it, you can achieve it; if you can dream it, you can become it. –William Arthur Ward

If you can imagine it, you can achieve it; if you can dream it, you can become it. –William Arthur Ward

Go confidently in the direction of your dreams. Live the life you have imagined. – Henry David Thoreau

Go confidently in the direction of your dreams. Live the life you have imagined. – Henry David Thoreau

Go confidently in the direction of your dreams. Live the life you have imagined. – Henry David Thoreau

Go confidently in the direction of your dreams. Live the life you have imagined. – Henry David Thoreau

Social Media ContentPlanner

Sunday	Monday	Tuesday	Wednesday	Thursday	Friday	Saturday

Week of:

Activities	MONDAY	TUESDAY	WEDNESDAY	THURSDAY	FRIDAY	SATURDAY	SUNDAY
TWO NEW PEOPLE New or memory jogger people. First time or reconnect.							
TWO NEW SHARES Share story, video, invite to group or event.							
TWO FOLLOW-UPS • Is this a good time to talk? • What did you like best about the info shared? • Are you ready to get started?							
TWO CUSTOMERS Customer Care Check-ins Add to FB group Referral Program							
SOCIAL MEDIA Post and comment (on your feed and in groups) 80/20 rule							
PERSONAL GROWTH Books, Audios, training call/zooms.							
TWO TEAM Connections and help with NEXT STEPS. Set up 3-way calls or zoom.							
Although the following may not occur daily, the more frequent they occur, the faster you will grow.							
EVENTS Promote an event. Host, attend, and/or present at an event.							
3-WAY CALL ZOOM Schedule, support, connect							
PRESENTING Your story, company, product, business							

Week of ____________

If you can imagine it, you can achieve it; if you can dream it, you can become it. —William Arthur Ward

If you can imagine it, you can achieve it; if you can dream it, you can become it. —William Arthur Ward

If you can imagine it, you can achieve it; if you can dream it, you can become it. —William Arthur Ward

If you can imagine it, you can achieve it; if you can dream it, you can become it. —William Arthur Ward

Go confidently in the direction of your dreams. Live the life you have imagined. – Henry David Thoreau

Go confidently in the direction of your dreams. Live the life you have imagined. – Henry David Thoreau

Go confidently in the direction of your dreams. Live the life you have imagined. – Henry David Thoreau

Go confidently in the direction of your dreams. Live the life you have imagined. – Henry David Thoreau

Social Media ContentPlanner

Sunday	Monday	Tuesday	Wednesday	Thursday	Friday	Saturday

Week of:

Activities	MONDAY	TUESDAY	WEDNESDAY	THURSDAY	FRIDAY	SATURDAY	SUNDAY
TWO NEW PEOPLE New or memory jogger people. First time or reconnect.							
TWO NEW SHARES Share story, video, invite to group or event.							
TWO FOLLOW-UPS • Is this a good time to talk? • What did you like best about the info shared? • Are you ready to get started?							
TWO CUSTOMERS Customer Care Check-ins Add to FB group Referral Program							
SOCIAL MEDIA Post and comment (on your feed and in groups) 80/20 rule							
PERSONAL GROWTH Books, Audios, training call/zooms.							
TWO TEAM Connections and help with NEXT STEPS. Set up 3-way calls or zoom.							
Although the following may not occur daily, the more frequent they occur, the faster you will grow.							
EVENTS Promote an event. Host, attend, and/or present at an event.							
3-WAY CALL ZOOM Schedule, support, connect							
PRESENTING Your story, company, product, business							

Week of ______________

If you can imagine it, you can achieve it; if you can dream it, you can become it. —William Arthur Ward

If you can imagine it, you can achieve it; if you can dream it, you can become it. —William Arthur Ward
If you can imagine it, you can achieve it; if you can dream it, you can become it. —William Arthur Ward
If you can imagine it, you can achieve it; if you can dream it, you can become it. —William Arthur Ward

Go confidently in the direction of your dreams. Live the life you have imagined. – Henry David Thoreau

Go confidently in the direction of your dreams. Live the life you have imagined. – Henry David Thoreau
Go confidently in the direction of your dreams. Live the life you have imagined. – Henry David Thoreau
Go confidently in the direction of your dreams. Live the life you have imagined. – Henry David Thoreau

Social Media ContentPlanner

Sunday	Monday	Tuesday	Wednesday	Thursday	Friday	Saturday

Week of:

Activities	MONDAY	TUESDAY	WEDNESDAY	THURSDAY	FRIDAY	SATURDAY	SUNDAY
TWO NEW PEOPLE New or memory jogger people. First time or reconnect.							
TWO NEW SHARES Share story, video, invite to group or event.							
TWO FOLLOW-UPS • Is this a good time to talk? • What did you like best about the info shared? • Are you ready to get started?							
TWO CUSTOMERS Customer Care Check-ins Add to FB group Referral Program							
SOCIAL MEDIA Post and comment (on your feed and in groups) 80/20 rule							
PERSONAL GROWTH Books, Audios, training call/zooms.							
TWO TEAM Connections and help with NEXT STEPS. Set up 3-way calls or zoom.							
Although the following may not occur daily, the more frequent they occur, the faster you will grow.							
EVENTS Promote an event. Host, attend, and/or present at an event.							
3-WAY CALL ZOOM Schedule, support, connect							
PRESENTING Your story, company, product, business							

Week of ____________

If you can imagine it, you can achieve it; if you can dream it, you can become it. —William Arthur Ward

If you can imagine it, you can achieve it; if you can dream it, you can become it. —William Arthur Ward

If you can imagine it, you can achieve it; if you can dream it, you can become it. —William Arthur Ward

If you can imagine it, you can achieve it; if you can dream it, you can become it. —William Arthur Ward

Go confidently in the direction of your dreams. Live the life you have imagined. – Henry David Thoreau

Go confidently in the direction of your dreams. Live the life you have imagined. – Henry David Thoreau

Go confidently in the direction of your dreams. Live the life you have imagined. – Henry David Thoreau

Go confidently in the direction of your dreams. Live the life you have imagined. – Henry David Thoreau

Social Media ContentPlanner

Sunday	Monday	Tuesday	Wednesday	Thursday	Friday	Saturday

Week of:

Activities	MONDAY	TUESDAY	WEDNESDAY	THURSDAY	FRIDAY	SATURDAY	SUNDAY
TWO NEW PEOPLE New or memory jogger people. First time or reconnect.							
TWO NEW SHARES Share story, video, invite to group or event.							
TWO FOLLOW-UPS • Is this a good time to talk? • What did you like best about the info shared? • Are you ready to get started?							
TWO CUSTOMERS Customer Care Check-ins Add to FB group Referral Program							
SOCIAL MEDIA Post and comment (on your feed and in groups) 80/20 rule							
PERSONAL GROWTH Books, Audios, training call/zooms.							
TWO TEAM Connections and help with NEXT STEPS. Set up 3-way calls or zoom.							
Although the following may not occur daily, the more frequent they occur, the faster you will grow.							
EVENTS Promote an event. Host, attend, and/or present at an event.							
3-WAY CALL ZOOM Schedule, support, connect							
PRESENTING Your story, company, product, business							

Week of ______________

If you can imagine it, you can achieve it; if you can dream it, you can become it. –William Arthur Ward

If you can imagine it, you can achieve it; if you can dream it, you can become it. –William Arthur Ward

If you can imagine it, you can achieve it; if you can dream it, you can become it. –William Arthur Ward

If you can imagine it, you can achieve it; if you can dream it, you can become it. –William Arthur Ward

Go confidently in the direction of your dreams. Live the life you have imagined. – Henry David Thoreau

Go confidently in the direction of your dreams. Live the life you have imagined. – Henry David Thoreau

Go confidently in the direction of your dreams. Live the life you have imagined. – Henry David Thoreau

Go confidently in the direction of your dreams. Live the life you have imagined. – Henry David Thoreau

Social Media ContentPlanner

Sunday	Monday	Tuesday	Wednesday	Thursday	Friday	Saturday

Week of:

Activities	MONDAY	TUESDAY	WEDNESDAY	THURSDAY	FRIDAY	SATURDAY	SUNDAY
TWO NEW PEOPLE New or memory jogger people. First time or reconnect.							
TWO NEW SHARES Share story, video, invite to group or event.							
TWO FOLLOW-UPS • Is this a good time to talk? • What did you like best about the info shared? • Are you ready to get started?							
TWO CUSTOMERS Customer Care Check-ins Add to FB group Referral Program							
SOCIAL MEDIA Post and comment (on your feed and in groups) 80/20 rule							
PERSONAL GROWTH Books, Audios, training call/zooms.							
TWO TEAM Connections and help with NEXT STEPS. Set up 3-way calls or zoom.							
Although the following may not occur daily, the more frequent they occur, the faster you will grow.							
EVENTS Promote an event. Host, attend, and/or present at an event.							
3-WAY CALL ZOOM Schedule, support, connect							
PRESENTING Your story, company, product, business							

Week of ____________

If you can imagine it, you can achieve it; if you can dream it, you can become it. –William Arthur Ward

If you can imagine it, you can achieve it; if you can dream it, you can become it. –William Arthur Ward

If you can imagine it, you can achieve it; if you can dream it, you can become it. –William Arthur Ward

If you can imagine it, you can achieve it; if you can dream it, you can become it. –William Arthur Ward

Go confidently in the direction of your dreams. Live the life you have imagined. – Henry David Thoreau

Go confidently in the direction of your dreams. Live the life you have imagined. – Henry David Thoreau

Go confidently in the direction of your dreams. Live the life you have imagined. – Henry David Thoreau

Go confidently in the direction of your dreams. Live the life you have imagined. – Henry David Thoreau

Social Media ContentPlanner

Sunday	Monday	Tuesday	Wednesday	Thursday	Friday	Saturday

Week of:

Activities	MONDAY	TUESDAY	WEDNESDAY	THURSDAY	FRIDAY	SATURDAY	SUNDAY
TWO NEW PEOPLE New or memory jogger people. First time or reconnect.							
TWO NEW SHARES Share story, video, invite to group or event.							
TWO FOLLOW-UPS • Is this a good time to talk? • What did you like best about the info shared? • Are you ready to get started?							
TWO CUSTOMERS Customer Care Check-ins Add to FB group Referral Program							
SOCIAL MEDIA Post and comment (on your feed and in groups) 80/20 rule							
PERSONAL GROWTH Books, Audios, training call/zooms.							
TWO TEAM Connections and help with NEXT STEPS. Set up 3-way calls or zoom.							
Although the following may not occur daily, the more frequent they occur, the faster you will grow.							
EVENTS Promote an event. Host, attend, and/or present at an event.							
3-WAY CALL ZOOM Schedule, support, connect							
PRESENTING Your story, company, product, business							

Week of ___________

If you can imagine it, you can achieve it; if you can dream it, you can become it. —William Arthur Ward

If you can imagine it, you can achieve it; if you can dream it, you can become it. —William Arthur Ward
If you can imagine it, you can achieve it; if you can dream it, you can become it. —William Arthur Ward
If you can imagine it, you can achieve it; if you can dream it, you can become it. —William Arthur Ward

Go confidently in the direction of your dreams. Live the life you have imagined. – Henry David Thoreau

Go confidently in the direction of your dreams. Live the life you have imagined. – Henry David Thoreau
Go confidently in the direction of your dreams. Live the life you have imagined. – Henry David Thoreau
Go confidently in the direction of your dreams. Live the life you have imagined. – Henry David Thoreau

Social Media ContentPlanner

Sunday	Monday	Tuesday	Wednesday	Thursday	Friday	Saturday

Week of:

Activities	MONDAY	TUESDAY	WEDNESDAY	THURSDAY	FRIDAY	SATURDAY	SUNDAY
TWO NEW PEOPLE New or memory jogger people. First time or reconnect.							
TWO NEW SHARES Share story, video, invite to group or event.							
TWO FOLLOW-UPS • Is this a good time to talk? • What did you like best about the info shared? • Are you ready to get started?							
TWO CUSTOMERS Customer Care Check-ins Add to FB group Referral Program							
SOCIAL MEDIA Post and comment (on your feed and in groups) 80/20 rule							
PERSONAL GROWTH Books, Audios, training call/zooms.							
TWO TEAM Connections and help with NEXT STEPS. Set up 3-way calls or zoom.							
Although the following may not occur daily, the more frequent they occur, the faster you will grow.							
EVENTS Promote an event. Host, attend, and/or present at an event.							
3-WAY CALL ZOOM Schedule, support, connect							
PRESENTING Your story, company, product, business							

Week of ______________

If you can imagine it, you can achieve it; if you can dream it, you can become it. —William Arthur Ward

If you can imagine it, you can achieve it; if you can dream it, you can become it. —William Arthur Ward
If you can imagine it, you can achieve it; if you can dream it, you can become it. —William Arthur Ward
If you can imagine it, you can achieve it; if you can dream it, you can become it. —William Arthur Ward

Go confidently in the direction of your dreams. Live the life you have imagined. – Henry David Thoreau

Go confidently in the direction of your dreams. Live the life you have imagined. – Henry David Thoreau
Go confidently in the direction of your dreams. Live the life you have imagined. – Henry David Thoreau
Go confidently in the direction of your dreams. Live the life you have imagined. – Henry David Thoreau

Social Media ContentPlanner

Sunday	Monday	Tuesday	Wednesday	Thursday	Friday	Saturday

Week of:

Activities	MONDAY	TUESDAY	WEDNESDAY	THURSDAY	FRIDAY	SATURDAY	SUNDAY
TWO NEW PEOPLE New or memory jogger people. First time or reconnect.							
TWO NEW SHARES Share story, video, invite to group or event.							
TWO FOLLOW-UPS • Is this a good time to talk? • What did you like best about the info shared? • Are you ready to get started?							
TWO CUSTOMERS Customer Care Check-ins Add to FB group Referral Program							
SOCIAL MEDIA Post and comment (on your feed and in groups) 80/20 rule							
PERSONAL GROWTH Books, Audios, training call/zooms.							
TWO TEAM Connections and help with NEXT STEPS. Set up 3-way calls or zoom.							
Although the following may not occur daily, the more frequent they occur, the faster you will grow.							
EVENTS Promote an event. Host, attend, and/or present at an event.							
3-WAY CALL ZOOM Schedule, support, connect							
PRESENTING Your story, company, product, business							

Week of ____________

If you can imagine it, you can achieve it; if you can dream it, you can become it. –William Arthur Ward

If you can imagine it, you can achieve it; if you can dream it, you can become it. –William Arthur Ward
If you can imagine it, you can achieve it; if you can dream it, you can become it. –William Arthur Ward
If you can imagine it, you can achieve it; if you can dream it, you can become it. –William Arthur Ward

Go confidently in the direction of your dreams. Live the life you have imagined. – Henry David Thoreau

Go confidently in the direction of your dreams. Live the life you have imagined. – Henry David Thoreau
Go confidently in the direction of your dreams. Live the life you have imagined. – Henry David Thoreau
Go confidently in the direction of your dreams. Live the life you have imagined. – Henry David Thoreau

Social Media ContentPlanner

Sunday	Monday	Tuesday	Wednesday	Thursday	Friday	Saturday

Week of:

Activities	MONDAY	TUESDAY	WEDNESDAY	THURSDAY	FRIDAY	SATURDAY	SUNDAY
TWO NEW PEOPLE New or memory jogger people. First time or reconnect.							
TWO NEW SHARES Share story, video, invite to group or event.							
TWO FOLLOW-UPS • Is this a good time to talk? • What did you like best about the info shared? • Are you ready to get started?							
TWO CUSTOMERS Customer Care Check-ins Add to FB group Referral Program							
SOCIAL MEDIA Post and comment (on your feed and in groups) 80/20 rule							
PERSONAL GROWTH Books, Audios, training call/zooms.							
TWO TEAM Connections and help with NEXT STEPS. Set up 3-way calls or zoom.							
Although the following may not occur daily, the more frequent they occur, the faster you will grow.							
EVENTS Promote an event. Host, attend, and/or present at an event.							
3-WAY CALL ZOOM Schedule, support, connect							
PRESENTING Your story, company, product, business							

Week of ____________

If you can imagine it, you can achieve it; if you can dream it, you can become it. – William Arthur Ward

If you can imagine it, you can achieve it; if you can dream it, you can become it. – William Arthur Ward
If you can imagine it, you can achieve it; if you can dream it, you can become it. – William Arthur Ward
If you can imagine it, you can achieve it; if you can dream it, you can become it. – William Arthur Ward

Go confidently in the direction of your dreams. Live the life you have imagined. – Henry David Thoreau

Go confidently in the direction of your dreams. Live the life you have imagined. – Henry David Thoreau
Go confidently in the direction of your dreams. Live the life you have imagined. – Henry David Thoreau
Go confidently in the direction of your dreams. Live the life you have imagined. – Henry David Thoreau

Social Media ContentPlanner

Sunday	Monday	Tuesday	Wednesday	Thursday	Friday	Saturday

Week of:

Activities	MONDAY	TUESDAY	WEDNESDAY	THURSDAY	FRIDAY	SATURDAY	SUNDAY
TWO NEW PEOPLE New or memory jogger people. First time or reconnect.							
TWO NEW SHARES Share story, video, invite to group or event.							
TWO FOLLOW-UPS • Is this a good time to talk? • What did you like best about the info shared? • Are you ready to get started?							
TWO CUSTOMERS Customer Care Check-ins Add to FB group Referral Program							
SOCIAL MEDIA Post and comment (on your feed and in groups) 80/20 rule							
PERSONAL GROWTH Books, Audios, training call/zooms.							
TWO TEAM Connections and help with NEXT STEPS. Set up 3-way calls or zoom.							
Although the following may not occur daily, the more frequent they occur, the faster you will grow.							
EVENTS Promote an event. Host, attend, and/or present at an event.							
3-WAY CALL ZOOM Schedule, support, connect							
PRESENTING Your story, company, product, business							

Week of ______________

If you can imagine it, you can achieve it; if you can dream it, you can become it. –William Arthur Ward
If you can imagine it, you can achieve it; if you can dream it, you can become it. –William Arthur Ward
If you can imagine it, you can achieve it; if you can dream it, you can become it. –William Arthur Ward
If you can imagine it, you can achieve it; if you can dream it, you can become it. –William Arthur Ward

Go confidently in the direction of your dreams. Live the life you have imagined. – Henry David Thoreau
Go confidently in the direction of your dreams. Live the life you have imagined. – Henry David Thoreau
Go confidently in the direction of your dreams. Live the life you have imagined. – Henry David Thoreau
Go confidently in the direction of your dreams. Live the life you have imagined. – Henry David Thoreau

Social Media ContentPlanner

Sunday	Monday	Tuesday	Wednesday	Thursday	Friday	Saturday

Week of:

Activities	MONDAY	TUESDAY	WEDNESDAY	THURSDAY	FRIDAY	SATURDAY	SUNDAY
TWO NEW PEOPLE New or memory jogger people. First time or reconnect.							
TWO NEW SHARES Share story, video, invite to group or event.							
TWO FOLLOW-UPS • Is this a good time to talk? • What did you like best about the info shared? • Are you ready to get started?							
TWO CUSTOMERS Customer Care Check-ins Add to FB group Referral Program							
SOCIAL MEDIA Post and comment (on your feed and in groups) 80/20 rule							
PERSONAL GROWTH Books, Audios, training call/zooms.							
TWO TEAM Connections and help with NEXT STEPS. Set up 3-way calls or zoom.							
Although the following may not occur daily, the more frequent they occur, the faster you will grow.							
EVENTS Promote an event. Host, attend, and/or present at an event.							
3-WAY CALL ZOOM Schedule, support, connect							
PRESENTING Your story, company, product, business							

Week of ______________

If you can imagine it, you can achieve it; if you can dream it, you can become it. —William Arthur Ward

If you can imagine it, you can achieve it; if you can dream it, you can become it. —William Arthur Ward

If you can imagine it, you can achieve it; if you can dream it, you can become it. —William Arthur Ward

If you can imagine it, you can achieve it; if you can dream it, you can become it. —William Arthur Ward

Go confidently in the direction of your dreams. Live the life you have imagined. – Henry David Thoreau

Go confidently in the direction of your dreams. Live the life you have imagined. – Henry David Thoreau

Go confidently in the direction of your dreams. Live the life you have imagined. – Henry David Thoreau

Go confidently in the direction of your dreams. Live the life you have imagined. – Henry David Thoreau

Social Media ContentPlanner

Sunday	Monday	Tuesday	Wednesday	Thursday	Friday	Saturday

Week of:

Activities	MONDAY	TUESDAY	WEDNESDAY	THURSDAY	FRIDAY	SATURDAY	SUNDAY
TWO NEW PEOPLE New or memory jogger people. First time or reconnect.							
TWO NEW SHARES Share story, video, invite to group or event.							
TWO FOLLOW-UPS • Is this a good time to talk? • What did you like best about the info shared? • Are you ready to get started?							
TWO CUSTOMERS Customer Care Check-ins Add to FB group Referral Program							
SOCIAL MEDIA Post and comment (on your feed and in groups) 80/20 rule							
PERSONAL GROWTH Books, Audios, training call/zooms.							
TWO TEAM Connections and help with NEXT STEPS. Set up 3-way calls or zoom.							
Although the following may not occur daily, the more frequent they occur, the faster you will grow.							
EVENTS Promote an event. Host, attend, and/or present at an event.							
3-WAY CALL ZOOM Schedule, support, connect							
PRESENTING Your story, company, product, business							

Week of ______________

If you can imagine it, you can achieve it; if you can dream it, you can become it. –William Arthur Ward

If you can imagine it, you can achieve it; if you can dream it, you can become it. –William Arthur Ward
If you can imagine it, you can achieve it; if you can dream it, you can become it. –William Arthur Ward
If you can imagine it, you can achieve it; if you can dream it, you can become it. –William Arthur Ward

Go confidently in the direction of your dreams. Live the life you have imagined. – Henry David Thoreau

Go confidently in the direction of your dreams. Live the life you have imagined. – Henry David Thoreau
Go confidently in the direction of your dreams. Live the life you have imagined. – Henry David Thoreau
Go confidently in the direction of your dreams. Live the life you have imagined. – Henry David Thoreau

Social Media ContentPlanner

Sunday	Monday	Tuesday	Wednesday	Thursday	Friday	Saturday

Week of:

Activities	MONDAY	TUESDAY	WEDNESDAY	THURSDAY	FRIDAY	SATURDAY	SUNDAY
TWO NEW PEOPLE New or memory jogger people. First time or reconnect.							
TWO NEW SHARES Share story, video, invite to group or event.							
TWO FOLLOW-UPS • Is this a good time to talk? • What did you like best about the info shared? • Are you ready to get started?							
TWO CUSTOMERS Customer Care Check-ins Add to FB group Referral Program							
SOCIAL MEDIA Post and comment (on your feed and in groups) 80/20 rule							
PERSONAL GROWTH Books, Audios, training call/zooms.							
TWO TEAM Connections and help with NEXT STEPS. Set up 3-way calls or zoom.							
Although the following may not occur daily, the more frequent they occur, the faster you will grow.							
EVENTS Promote an event. Host, attend, and/or present at an event.							
3-WAY CALL ZOOM Schedule, support, connect							
PRESENTING Your story, company, product, business							

Week of ____________

If you can imagine it, you can achieve it; if you can dream it, you can become it. –William Arthur Ward

If you can imagine it, you can achieve it; if you can dream it, you can become it. –William Arthur Ward

If you can imagine it, you can achieve it; if you can dream it, you can become it. –William Arthur Ward

If you can imagine it, you can achieve it; if you can dream it, you can become it. –William Arthur Ward

Go confidently in the direction of your dreams. Live the life you have imagined. – Henry David Thoreau

Go confidently in the direction of your dreams. Live the life you have imagined. – Henry David Thoreau

Go confidently in the direction of your dreams. Live the life you have imagined. – Henry David Thoreau

Go confidently in the direction of your dreams. Live the life you have imagined. – Henry David Thoreau

Social Media ContentPlanner

Sunday	Monday	Tuesday	Wednesday	Thursday	Friday	Saturday

Week of:

Activities	MONDAY	TUESDAY	WEDNESDAY	THURSDAY	FRIDAY	SATURDAY	SUNDAY
TWO NEW PEOPLE New or memory jogger people. First time or reconnect.							
TWO NEW SHARES Share story, video, invite to group or event.							
TWO FOLLOW-UPS • Is this a good time to talk? • What did you like best about the info shared? • Are you ready to get started?							
TWO CUSTOMERS Customer Care Check-ins Add to FB group Referral Program							
SOCIAL MEDIA Post and comment (on your feed and in groups) 80/20 rule							
PERSONAL GROWTH Books, Audios, training call/zooms.							
TWO TEAM Connections and help with NEXT STEPS. Set up 3-way calls or zoom.							
Although the following may not occur daily, the more frequent they occur, the faster you will grow.							
EVENTS Promote an event. Host, attend, and/or present at an event.							
3-WAY CALL ZOOM Schedule, support, connect							
PRESENTING Your story, company, product, business							

Week of ____________

If you can imagine it, you can achieve it; if you can dream it, you can become it. –William Arthur Ward

If you can imagine it, you can achieve it; if you can dream it, you can become it. –William Arthur Ward

If you can imagine it, you can achieve it; if you can dream it, you can become it. –William Arthur Ward

If you can imagine it, you can achieve it; if you can dream it, you can become it. –William Arthur Ward

Go confidently in the direction of your dreams. Live the life you have imagined. – Henry David Thoreau

Go confidently in the direction of your dreams. Live the life you have imagined. – Henry David Thoreau

Go confidently in the direction of your dreams. Live the life you have imagined. – Henry David Thoreau

Go confidently in the direction of your dreams. Live the life you have imagined. – Henry David Thoreau

Social Media ContentPlanner

Sunday	Monday	Tuesday	Wednesday	Thursday	Friday	Saturday

Week of:

Activities	MONDAY	TUESDAY	WEDNESDAY	THURSDAY	FRIDAY	SATURDAY	SUNDAY
TWO NEW PEOPLE New or memory jogger people. First time or reconnect.							
TWO NEW SHARES Share story, video, invite to group or event.							
TWO FOLLOW-UPS • Is this a good time to talk? • What did you like best about the info shared? • Are you ready to get started?							
TWO CUSTOMERS Customer Care Check-ins Add to FB group Referral Program							
SOCIAL MEDIA Post and comment (on your feed and in groups) 80/20 rule							
PERSONAL GROWTH Books, Audios, training call/zooms.							
TWO TEAM Connections and help with NEXT STEPS. Set up 3-way calls or zoom.							
Although the following may not occur daily, the more frequent they occur, the faster you will grow.							
EVENTS Promote an event. Host, attend, and/or present at an event.							
3-WAY CALL ZOOM Schedule, support, connect							
PRESENTING Your story, company, product, business							

Week of ____________

If you can imagine it, you can achieve it; if you can dream it, you can become it. – William Arthur Ward

If you can imagine it, you can achieve it; if you can dream it, you can become it. – William Arthur Ward
If you can imagine it, you can achieve it; if you can dream it, you can become it. – William Arthur Ward
If you can imagine it, you can achieve it; if you can dream it, you can become it. – William Arthur Ward

Go confidently in the direction of your dreams. Live the life you have imagined. – Henry David Thoreau

Go confidently in the direction of your dreams. Live the life you have imagined. – Henry David Thoreau
Go confidently in the direction of your dreams. Live the life you have imagined. – Henry David Thoreau
Go confidently in the direction of your dreams. Live the life you have imagined. – Henry David Thoreau

Social Media ContentPlanner

Sunday	Monday	Tuesday	Wednesday	Thursday	Friday	Saturday

Week of:

Activities	MONDAY	TUESDAY	WEDNESDAY	THURSDAY	FRIDAY	SATURDAY	SUNDAY
TWO NEW PEOPLE New or memory jogger people. First time or reconnect.							
TWO NEW SHARES Share story, video, invite to group or event.							
TWO FOLLOW-UPS • Is this a good time to talk? • What did you like best about the info shared? • Are you ready to get started?							
TWO CUSTOMERS Customer Care Check-ins Add to FB group Referral Program							
SOCIAL MEDIA Post and comment (on your feed and in groups) 80/20 rule							
PERSONAL GROWTH Books, Audios, training call/zooms.							
TWO TEAM Connections and help with NEXT STEPS. Set up 3-way calls or zoom.							
Although the following may not occur daily, the more frequent they occur, the faster you will grow.							
EVENTS Promote an event. Host, attend, and/or present at an event.							
3-WAY CALL ZOOM Schedule, support, connect							
PRESENTING Your story, company, product, business							

Week of ____________

If you can imagine it, you can achieve it; if you can dream it, you can become it. – William Arthur Ward

If you can imagine it, you can achieve it; if you can dream it, you can become it. – William Arthur Ward

If you can imagine it, you can achieve it; if you can dream it, you can become it. – William Arthur Ward

If you can imagine it, you can achieve it; if you can dream it, you can become it. – William Arthur Ward

Go confidently in the direction of your dreams. Live the life you have imagined. – Henry David Thoreau

Go confidently in the direction of your dreams. Live the life you have imagined. – Henry David Thoreau

Go confidently in the direction of your dreams. Live the life you have imagined. – Henry David Thoreau

Go confidently in the direction of your dreams. Live the life you have imagined. – Henry David Thoreau

Social Media ContentPlanner

Sunday	Monday	Tuesday	Wednesday	Thursday	Friday	Saturday

Week of:

Activities	MONDAY	TUESDAY	WEDNESDAY	THURSDAY	FRIDAY	SATURDAY	SUNDAY
TWO NEW PEOPLE New or memory jogger people. First time or reconnect.							
TWO NEW SHARES Share story, video, invite to group or event.							
TWO FOLLOW-UPS • Is this a good time to talk? • What did you like best about the info shared? • Are you ready to get started?							
TWO CUSTOMERS Customer Care Check-ins Add to FB group Referral Program							
SOCIAL MEDIA Post and comment (on your feed and in groups) 80/20 rule							
PERSONAL GROWTH Books, Audios, training call/zooms.							
TWO TEAM Connections and help with NEXT STEPS. Set up 3-way calls or zoom.							
Although the following may not occur daily, the more frequent they occur, the faster you will grow.							
EVENTS Promote an event. Host, attend, and/or present at an event.							
3-WAY CALL ZOOM Schedule, support, connect							
PRESENTING Your story, company, product, business							

Week of ______________

If you can imagine it, you can achieve it; if you can dream it, you can become it. —William Arthur Ward

If you can imagine it, you can achieve it; if you can dream it, you can become it. —William Arthur Ward

If you can imagine it, you can achieve it; if you can dream it, you can become it. —William Arthur Ward

If you can imagine it, you can achieve it; if you can dream it, you can become it. —William Arthur Ward

Go confidently in the direction of your dreams. Live the life you have imagined. – Henry David Thoreau

Go confidently in the direction of your dreams. Live the life you have imagined. – Henry David Thoreau

Go confidently in the direction of your dreams. Live the life you have imagined. – Henry David Thoreau

Go confidently in the direction of your dreams. Live the life you have imagined. – Henry David Thoreau

Social Media ContentPlanner

Sunday	Monday	Tuesday	Wednesday	Thursday	Friday	Saturday

Week of:

Activities	MONDAY	TUESDAY	WEDNESDAY	THURSDAY	FRIDAY	SATURDAY	SUNDAY
TWO NEW PEOPLE New or memory jogger people. First time or reconnect.							
TWO NEW SHARES Share story, video, invite to group or event.							
TWO FOLLOW-UPS • Is this a good time to talk? • What did you like best about the info shared? • Are you ready to get started?							
TWO CUSTOMERS Customer Care Check-ins Add to FB group Referral Program							
SOCIAL MEDIA Post and comment (on your feed and in groups) 80/20 rule							
PERSONAL GROWTH Books, Audios, training call/zooms.							
TWO TEAM Connections and help with NEXT STEPS. Set up 3-way calls or zoom.							
Although the following may not occur daily, the more frequent they occur, the faster you will grow.							
EVENTS Promote an event. Host, attend, and/or present at an event.							
3-WAY CALL ZOOM Schedule, support, connect							
PRESENTING Your story, company, product, business							

Week of ____________

If you can imagine it, you can achieve it. If you can dream it, you can become it. – William Arthur Ward

If you can imagine it, you can achieve it. If you can dream it, you can become it. – William Arthur Ward

If you can imagine it, you can achieve it. If you can dream it, you can become it. – William Arthur Ward

If you can imagine it, you can achieve it. If you can dream it, you can become it. – William Arthur Ward

Go confidently in the direction of your dreams. Live the life you have imagined. – Henry David Thoreau

Go confidently in the direction of your dreams. Live the life you have imagined. – Henry David Thoreau

Go confidently in the direction of your dreams. Live the life you have imagined. – Henry David Thoreau

Go confidently in the direction of your dreams. Live the life you have imagined. – Henry David Thoreau

Social Media ContentPlanner

Sunday	Monday	Tuesday	Wednesday	Thursday	Friday	Saturday

Week of:

Activities	MONDAY	TUESDAY	WEDNESDAY	THURSDAY	FRIDAY	SATURDAY	SUNDAY
TWO NEW PEOPLE New or memory jogger people. First time or reconnect.							
TWO NEW SHARES Share story, video, invite to group or event.							
TWO FOLLOW-UPS • Is this a good time to talk? • What did you like best about the info shared? • Are you ready to get started?							
TWO CUSTOMERS Customer Care Check-ins Add to FB group Referral Program							
SOCIAL MEDIA Post and comment (on your feed and in groups) 80/20 rule							
PERSONAL GROWTH Books, Audios, training call/zooms.							
TWO TEAM Connections and help with NEXT STEPS. Set up 3-way calls or zoom.							
Although the following may not occur daily, the more frequent they occur, the faster you will grow.							
EVENTS Promote an event. Host, attend, and/or present at an event.							
3-WAY CALL ZOOM Schedule, support, connect							
PRESENTING Your story, company, product, business							

Week of ______________

If you can imagine it, you can achieve it; if you can dream it, you can become it. – William Arthur Ward

If you can imagine it, you can achieve it; if you can dream it, you can become it. – William Arthur Ward

If you can imagine it, you can achieve it; if you can dream it, you can become it. – William Arthur Ward

If you can imagine it, you can achieve it; if you can dream it, you can become it. – William Arthur Ward

Go confidently in the direction of your dreams. Live the life you have imagined. – Henry David Thoreau

Go confidently in the direction of your dreams. Live the life you have imagined. – Henry David Thoreau

Go confidently in the direction of your dreams. Live the life you have imagined. – Henry David Thoreau

Go confidently in the direction of your dreams. Live the life you have imagined. – Henry David Thoreau

Social Media Content Planner

Sunday	Monday	Tuesday	Wednesday	Thursday	Friday	Saturday

Week of:

Activities	MONDAY	TUESDAY	WEDNESDAY	THURSDAY	FRIDAY	SATURDAY	SUNDAY
TWO NEW PEOPLE New or memory jogger people. First time or reconnect.							
TWO NEW SHARES Share story, video, invite to group or event.							
TWO FOLLOW-UPS • Is this a good time to talk? • What did you like best about the info shared? • Are you ready to get started?							
TWO CUSTOMERS Customer Care Check-ins Add to FB group Referral Program							
SOCIAL MEDIA Post and comment (on your feed and in groups) 80/20 rule							
PERSONAL GROWTH Books, Audios, training call/zooms.							
TWO TEAM Connections and help with NEXT STEPS. Set up 3-way calls or zoom.							
Although the following may not occur daily, the more frequent they occur, the faster you will grow.							
EVENTS Promote an event. Host, attend, and/or present at an event.							
3-WAY CALL ZOOM Schedule, support, connect							
PRESENTING Your story, company, product, business							

Week of ____________

If you can imagine it, you can achieve it. If you can dream it, you can become it. —William Arthur Ward

If you can imagine it, you can achieve it. If you can dream it, you can become it. —William Arthur Ward

If you can imagine it, you can achieve it. If you can dream it, you can become it. —William Arthur Ward

If you can imagine it, you can achieve it. If you can dream it, you can become it. —William Arthur Ward

Go confidently in the direction of your dreams. Live the life you have imagined. – Henry David Thoreau

Go confidently in the direction of your dreams. Live the life you have imagined. – Henry David Thoreau

Go confidently in the direction of your dreams. Live the life you have imagined. – Henry David Thoreau

Go confidently in the direction of your dreams. Live the life you have imagined. – Henry David Thoreau

Social Media ContentPlanner

Sunday	Monday	Tuesday	Wednesday	Thursday	Friday	Saturday

Week of:

Activities	MONDAY	TUESDAY	WEDNESDAY	THURSDAY	FRIDAY	SATURDAY	SUNDAY
TWO NEW PEOPLE New or memory jogger people. First time or reconnect.							
TWO NEW SHARES Share story, video, invite to group or event.							
TWO FOLLOW-UPS • Is this a good time to talk? • What did you like best about the info shared? • Are you ready to get started?							
TWO CUSTOMERS Customer Care Check-ins Add to FB group Referral Program							
SOCIAL MEDIA Post and comment (on your feed and in groups) 80/20 rule							
PERSONAL GROWTH Books, Audios, training call/zooms.							
TWO TEAM Connections and help with NEXT STEPS. Set up 3-way calls or zoom.							
Although the following may not occur daily, the more frequent they occur, the faster you will grow.							
EVENTS Promote an event. Host, attend, and/or present at an event.							
3-WAY CALL ZOOM Schedule, support, connect							
PRESENTING Your story, company, product, business							

Week of ______________

If you can imagine it, you can achieve it; if you can dream it, you can become it. –William Arthur Ward

If you can imagine it, you can achieve it; if you can dream it, you can become it. –William Arthur Ward

If you can imagine it, you can achieve it; if you can dream it, you can become it. –William Arthur Ward

If you can imagine it, you can achieve it; if you can dream it, you can become it. –William Arthur Ward

Go confidently in the direction of your dreams. Live the life you have imagined. – Henry David Thoreau

Go confidently in the direction of your dreams. Live the life you have imagined. – Henry David Thoreau

Go confidently in the direction of your dreams. Live the life you have imagined. – Henry David Thoreau

Go confidently in the direction of your dreams. Live the life you have imagined. – Henry David Thoreau

Social Media ContentPlanner

Sunday	Monday	Tuesday	Wednesday	Thursday	Friday	Saturday

Week of:

Activities	MONDAY	TUESDAY	WEDNESDAY	THURSDAY	FRIDAY	SATURDAY	SUNDAY
TWO NEW PEOPLE New or memory jogger people. First time or reconnect.							
TWO NEW SHARES Share story, video, invite to group or event.							
TWO FOLLOW-UPS • Is this a good time to talk? • What did you like best about the info shared? • Are you ready to get started?							
TWO CUSTOMERS Customer Care Check-ins Add to FB group Referral Program							
SOCIAL MEDIA Post and comment (on your feed and in groups) 80/20 rule							
PERSONAL GROWTH Books, Audios, training call/zooms.							
TWO TEAM Connections and help with NEXT STEPS. Set up 3-way calls or zoom.							
Although the following may not occur daily, the more frequent they occur, the faster you will grow.							
EVENTS Promote an event. Host, attend, and/or present at an event.							
3-WAY CALL ZOOM Schedule, support, connect							
PRESENTING Your story, company, product, business							

Week of ______________

If you can imagine it, you can achieve it; if you can dream it, you can become it. –William Arthur Ward

If you can imagine it, you can achieve it; if you can dream it, you can become it. –William Arthur Ward

If you can imagine it, you can achieve it; if you can dream it, you can become it. –William Arthur Ward

If you can imagine it, you can achieve it; if you can dream it, you can become it. –William Arthur Ward

Go confidently in the direction of your dreams. Live the life you have imagined. – Henry David Thoreau

Go confidently in the direction of your dreams. Live the life you have imagined. – Henry David Thoreau

Go confidently in the direction of your dreams. Live the life you have imagined. – Henry David Thoreau

Go confidently in the direction of your dreams. Live the life you have imagined. – Henry David Thoreau

Social Media ContentPlanner

Sunday	Monday	Tuesday	Wednesday	Thursday	Friday	Saturday

Week of:

Activities	MONDAY	TUESDAY	WEDNESDAY	THURSDAY	FRIDAY	SATURDAY	SUNDAY
TWO NEW PEOPLE New or memory jogger people. First time or reconnect.							
TWO NEW SHARES Share story, video, invite to group or event.							
TWO FOLLOW-UPS • Is this a good time to talk? • What did you like best about the info shared? • Are you ready to get started?							
TWO CUSTOMERS Customer Care Check-ins Add to FB group Referral Program							
SOCIAL MEDIA Post and comment (on your feed and in groups) 80/20 rule							
PERSONAL GROWTH Books, Audios, training call/zooms.							
TWO TEAM Connections and help with NEXT STEPS. Set up 3-way calls or zoom.							
Although the following may not occur daily, the more frequent they occur, the faster you will grow.							
EVENTS Promote an event. Host, attend, and/or present at an event.							
3-WAY CALL ZOOM Schedule, support, connect							
PRESENTING Your story, company, product, business							

Week of ____________

If you can imagine it, you can achieve it; if you can dream it, you can become it. –William Arthur Ward

Go confidently in the direction of your dreams. Live the life you have imagined. – Henry David Thoreau

Social Media ContentPlanner

Sunday	Monday	Tuesday	Wednesday	Thursday	Friday	Saturday

Week of:

Activities	MONDAY	TUESDAY	WEDNESDAY	THURSDAY	FRIDAY	SATURDAY	SUNDAY
TWO NEW PEOPLE New or memory jogger people. First time or reconnect.							
TWO NEW SHARES Share story, video, invite to group or event.							
TWO FOLLOW-UPS • Is this a good time to talk? • What did you like best about the info shared? • Are you ready to get started?							
TWO CUSTOMERS Customer Care Check-ins Add to FB group Referral Program							
SOCIAL MEDIA Post and comment (on your feed and in groups) 80/20 rule							
PERSONAL GROWTH Books, Audios, training call/zooms.							
TWO TEAM Connections and help with NEXT STEPS. Set up 3-way calls or zoom.							
Although the following may not occur daily, the more frequent they occur, the faster you will grow.							
EVENTS Promote an event. Host, attend, and/or present at an event.							
3-WAY CALL ZOOM Schedule, support, connect							
PRESENTING Your story, company, product, business							

Week of ____________

If you can imagine it, you can achieve it. If you can dream it, you can become it. –William Arthur Ward

If you can imagine it, you can achieve it. If you can dream it, you can become it. –William Arthur Ward
If you can imagine it, you can achieve it. If you can dream it, you can become it. –William Arthur Ward
If you can imagine it, you can achieve it. If you can dream it, you can become it. –William Arthur Ward

Go confidently in the direction of your dreams. Live the life you have imagined. – Henry David Thoreau

Go confidently in the direction of your dreams. Live the life you have imagined. – Henry David Thoreau
Go confidently in the direction of your dreams. Live the life you have imagined. – Henry David Thoreau
Go confidently in the direction of your dreams. Live the life you have imagined. – Henry David Thoreau

Social Media ContentPlanner

Sunday	Monday	Tuesday	Wednesday	Thursday	Friday	Saturday

Week of:

Activities	MONDAY	TUESDAY	WEDNESDAY	THURSDAY	FRIDAY	SATURDAY	SUNDAY
TWO NEW PEOPLE New or memory jogger people. First time or reconnect.							
TWO NEW SHARES Share story, video, invite to group or event.							
TWO FOLLOW-UPS • Is this a good time to talk? • What did you like best about the info shared? • Are you ready to get started?							
TWO CUSTOMERS Customer Care Check-ins Add to FB group Referral Program							
SOCIAL MEDIA Post and comment (on your feed and in groups) 80/20 rule							
PERSONAL GROWTH Books, Audios, training call/zooms.							
TWO TEAM Connections and help with NEXT STEPS. Set up 3-way calls or zoom.							
Although the following may not occur daily, the more frequent they occur, the faster you will grow.							
EVENTS Promote an event. Host, attend, and/or present at an event.							
3-WAY CALL ZOOM Schedule, support, connect							
PRESENTING Your story, company, product, business							

Week of ____________

If you can imagine it, you can achieve it; if you can dream it, you can become it. –William Arthur Ward

If you can imagine it, you can achieve it; if you can dream it, you can become it. –William Arthur Ward
If you can imagine it, you can achieve it; if you can dream it, you can become it. –William Arthur Ward
If you can imagine it, you can achieve it; if you can dream it, you can become it. –William Arthur Ward

Go confidently in the direction of your dreams. Live the life you have imagined. – Henry David Thoreau

Go confidently in the direction of your dreams. Live the life you have imagined. – Henry David Thoreau
Go confidently in the direction of your dreams. Live the life you have imagined. – Henry David Thoreau
Go confidently in the direction of your dreams. Live the life you have imagined. – Henry David Thoreau

Social Media ContentPlanner

Sunday	Monday	Tuesday	Wednesday	Thursday	Friday	Saturday

Week of:

Activities	MONDAY	TUESDAY	WEDNESDAY	THURSDAY	FRIDAY	SATURDAY	SUNDAY
TWO NEW PEOPLE New or memory jogger people. First time or reconnect.							
TWO NEW SHARES Share story, video, invite to group or event.							
TWO FOLLOW-UPS • Is this a good time to talk? • What did you like best about the info shared? • Are you ready to get started?							
TWO CUSTOMERS Customer Care Check-ins Add to FB group Referral Program							
SOCIAL MEDIA Post and comment (on your feed and in groups) 80/20 rule							
PERSONAL GROWTH Books, Audios, training call/zooms.							
TWO TEAM Connections and help with NEXT STEPS. Set up 3-way calls or zoom.							
Although the following may not occur daily, the more frequent they occur, the faster you will grow.							
EVENTS Promote an event. Host, attend, and/or present at an event.							
3-WAY CALL ZOOM Schedule, support, connect							
PRESENTING Your story, company, product, business							

Week of ____________

If you can imagine it, you can achieve it; if you can dream it, you can become it. –William Arthur Ward

If you can imagine it, you can achieve it; if you can dream it, you can become it. –William Arthur Ward
If you can imagine it, you can achieve it; if you can dream it, you can become it. –William Arthur Ward
If you can imagine it, you can achieve it; if you can dream it, you can become it. –William Arthur Ward

Go confidently in the direction of your dreams. Live the life you have imagined. – Henry David Thoreau

Go confidently in the direction of your dreams. Live the life you have imagined. – Henry David Thoreau
Go confidently in the direction of your dreams. Live the life you have imagined. – Henry David Thoreau
Go confidently in the direction of your dreams. Live the life you have imagined. – Henry David Thoreau

Social Media ContentPlanner

Sunday	Monday	Tuesday	Wednesday	Thursday	Friday	Saturday

Week of:

Activities	MONDAY	TUESDAY	WEDNESDAY	THURSDAY	FRIDAY	SATURDAY	SUNDAY
TWO NEW PEOPLE New or memory jogger people. First time or reconnect.							
TWO NEW SHARES Share story, video, invite to group or event.							
TWO FOLLOW-UPS • Is this a good time to talk? • What did you like best about the info shared? • Are you ready to get started?							
TWO CUSTOMERS Customer Care Check-ins Add to FB group Referral Program							
SOCIAL MEDIA Post and comment (on your feed and in groups) 80/20 rule							
PERSONAL GROWTH Books, Audios, training call/zooms.							
TWO TEAM Connections and help with NEXT STEPS. Set up 3-way calls or zoom.							
Although the following may not occur daily, the more frequent they occur, the faster you will grow.							
EVENTS Promote an event. Host, attend, and/or present at an event.							
3-WAY CALL ZOOM Schedule, support, connect							
PRESENTING Your story, company, product, business							

Week of ______________

If you can imagine it, you can achieve it; if you can dream it, you can become it. —William Arthur Ward

If you can imagine it, you can achieve it; if you can dream it, you can become it. —William Arthur Ward

If you can imagine it, you can achieve it; if you can dream it, you can become it. —William Arthur Ward

If you can imagine it, you can achieve it; if you can dream it, you can become it. —William Arthur Ward

Go confidently in the direction of your dreams. Live the life you have imagined. – Henry David Thoreau

Go confidently in the direction of your dreams. Live the life you have imagined. – Henry David Thoreau

Go confidently in the direction of your dreams. Live the life you have imagined. – Henry David Thoreau

Go confidently in the direction of your dreams. Live the life you have imagined. – Henry David Thoreau

Social Media ContentPlanner

Sunday	Monday	Tuesday	Wednesday	Thursday	Friday	Saturday

Week of:

Activities	MONDAY	TUESDAY	WEDNESDAY	THURSDAY	FRIDAY	SATURDAY	SUNDAY
TWO NEW PEOPLE New or memory jogger people. First time or reconnect.							
TWO NEW SHARES Share story, video, invite to group or event.							
TWO FOLLOW-UPS • Is this a good time to talk? • What did you like best about the info shared? • Are you ready to get started?							
TWO CUSTOMERS Customer Care Check-ins Add to FB group Referral Program							
SOCIAL MEDIA Post and comment (on your feed and in groups) 80/20 rule							
PERSONAL GROWTH Books, Audios, training call/zooms.							
TWO TEAM Connections and help with NEXT STEPS. Set up 3-way calls or zoom.							
Although the following may not occur daily, the more frequent they occur, the faster you will grow.							
EVENTS Promote an event. Host, attend, and/or present at an event.							
3-WAY CALL ZOOM Schedule, support, connect							
PRESENTING Your story, company, product, business							

Week of ______________

If you can imagine it, you can achieve it; if you can dream it, you can become it. – William Arthur Ward

If you can imagine it, you can achieve it; if you can dream it, you can become it. – William Arthur Ward
If you can imagine it, you can achieve it; if you can dream it, you can become it. – William Arthur Ward
If you can imagine it, you can achieve it; if you can dream it, you can become it. – William Arthur Ward

Go confidently in the direction of your dreams. Live the life you have imagined. – Henry David Thoreau

Go confidently in the direction of your dreams. Live the life you have imagined. – Henry David Thoreau
Go confidently in the direction of your dreams. Live the life you have imagined. – Henry David Thoreau
Go confidently in the direction of your dreams. Live the life you have imagined. – Henry David Thoreau

Social Media ContentPlanner

Sunday	Monday	Tuesday	Wednesday	Thursday	Friday	Saturday

Week of:

Activities	MONDAY	TUESDAY	WEDNESDAY	THURSDAY	FRIDAY	SATURDAY	SUNDAY
TWO NEW PEOPLE New or memory jogger people. First time or reconnect.							
TWO NEW SHARES Share story, video, invite to group or event.							
TWO FOLLOW-UPS • Is this a good time to talk? • What did you like best about the info shared? • Are you ready to get started?							
TWO CUSTOMERS Customer Care Check-ins Add to FB group Referral Program							
SOCIAL MEDIA Post and comment (on your feed and in groups) 80/20 rule							
PERSONAL GROWTH Books, Audios, training call/zooms.							
TWO TEAM Connections and help with NEXT STEPS. Set up 3-way calls or zoom.							
Although the following may not occur daily, the more frequent they occur, the faster you will grow.							
EVENTS Promote an event. Host, attend, and/or present at an event.							
3-WAY CALL ZOOM Schedule, support, connect							
PRESENTING Your story, company, product, business							

Week of ______________

If you can imagine it, you can achieve it; if you can dream it, you can become it. –William Arthur Ward

If you can imagine it, you can achieve it; if you can dream it, you can become it. –William Arthur Ward
If you can imagine it, you can achieve it; if you can dream it, you can become it. –William Arthur Ward
If you can imagine it, you can achieve it; if you can dream it, you can become it. –William Arthur Ward

Go confidently in the direction of your dreams. Live the life you have imagined. – Henry David Thoreau

Go confidently in the direction of your dreams. Live the life you have imagined. – Henry David Thoreau
Go confidently in the direction of your dreams. Live the life you have imagined. – Henry David Thoreau
Go confidently in the direction of your dreams. Live the life you have imagined. – Henry David Thoreau

Social Media ContentPlanner

Sunday	Monday	Tuesday	Wednesday	Thursday	Friday	Saturday

Week of:

Activities	MONDAY	TUESDAY	WEDNESDAY	THURSDAY	FRIDAY	SATURDAY	SUNDAY
TWO NEW PEOPLE New or memory jogger people. First time or reconnect.							
TWO NEW SHARES Share story, video, invite to group or event.							
TWO FOLLOW-UPS • Is this a good time to talk? • What did you like best about the info shared? • Are you ready to get started?							
TWO CUSTOMERS Customer Care Check-ins Add to FB group Referral Program							
SOCIAL MEDIA Post and comment (on your feed and in groups) 80/20 rule							
PERSONAL GROWTH Books, Audios, training call/zooms.							
TWO TEAM Connections and help with NEXT STEPS. Set up 3-way calls or zoom.							
Although the following may not occur daily, the more frequent they occur, the faster you will grow.							
EVENTS Promote an event. Host, attend, and/or present at an event.							
3-WAY CALL ZOOM Schedule, support, connect							
PRESENTING Your story, company, product, business							

Week of ____________

If you can imagine it, you can achieve it; if you can dream it, you can become it. –William Arthur Ward

If you can imagine it, you can achieve it; if you can dream it, you can become it. –William Arthur Ward

If you can imagine it, you can achieve it; if you can dream it, you can become it. –William Arthur Ward

If you can imagine it, you can achieve it; if you can dream it, you can become it. –William Arthur Ward

Go confidently in the direction of your dreams. Live the life you have imagined. – Henry David Thoreau

Go confidently in the direction of your dreams. Live the life you have imagined. – Henry David Thoreau

Go confidently in the direction of your dreams. Live the life you have imagined. – Henry David Thoreau

Go confidently in the direction of your dreams. Live the life you have imagined. – Henry David Thoreau

Social Media ContentPlanner

Sunday	Monday	Tuesday	Wednesday	Thursday	Friday	Saturday

Week of:

Activities	MONDAY	TUESDAY	WEDNESDAY	THURSDAY	FRIDAY	SATURDAY	SUNDAY
TWO NEW PEOPLE New or memory jogger people. First time or reconnect.							
TWO NEW SHARES Share story, video, invite to group or event.							
TWO FOLLOW-UPS • Is this a good time to talk? • What did you like best about the info shared? • Are you ready to get started?							
TWO CUSTOMERS Customer Care Check-ins Add to FB group Referral Program							
SOCIAL MEDIA Post and comment (on your feed and in groups) 80/20 rule							
PERSONAL GROWTH Books, Audios, training call/zooms.							
TWO TEAM Connections and help with NEXT STEPS. Set up 3-way calls or zoom.							
Although the following may not occur daily, the more frequent they occur, the faster you will grow.							
EVENTS Promote an event. Host, attend, and/or present at an event.							
3-WAY CALL ZOOM Schedule, support, connect							
PRESENTING Your story, company, product, business							

Week of ______________

If you can imagine it, you can achieve it; if you can dream it, you can become it. —William Arthur Ward

If you can imagine it, you can achieve it; if you can dream it, you can become it. —William Arthur Ward
If you can imagine it, you can achieve it; if you can dream it, you can become it. —William Arthur Ward
If you can imagine it, you can achieve it; if you can dream it, you can become it. —William Arthur Ward

Go confidently in the direction of your dreams. Live the life you have imagined. – Henry David Thoreau

Go confidently in the direction of your dreams. Live the life you have imagined. – Henry David Thoreau
Go confidently in the direction of your dreams. Live the life you have imagined. – Henry David Thoreau
Go confidently in the direction of your dreams. Live the life you have imagined. – Henry David Thoreau

Social Media ContentPlanner

Sunday	Monday	Tuesday	Wednesday	Thursday	Friday	Saturday

Week of:

Activities	MONDAY	TUESDAY	WEDNESDAY	THURSDAY	FRIDAY	SATURDAY	SUNDAY
TWO NEW PEOPLE New or memory jogger people. First time or reconnect.							
TWO NEW SHARES Share story, video, invite to group or event.							
TWO FOLLOW-UPS • Is this a good time to talk? • What did you like best about the info shared? • Are you ready to get started?							
TWO CUSTOMERS Customer Care Check-ins Add to FB group Referral Program							
SOCIAL MEDIA Post and comment (on your feed and in groups) 80/20 rule							
PERSONAL GROWTH Books, Audios, training call/zooms.							
TWO TEAM Connections and help with NEXT STEPS. Set up 3-way calls or zoom.							
Although the following may not occur daily, the more frequent they occur, the faster you will grow.							
EVENTS Promote an event. Host, attend, and/or present at an event.							
3-WAY CALL ZOOM Schedule, support, connect							
PRESENTING Your story, company, product, business							

Week of ___________

If you can imagine it, you can achieve it; if you can dream it, you can become it. – William Arthur Ward

If you can imagine it, you can achieve it; if you can dream it, you can become it. – William Arthur Ward

If you can imagine it, you can achieve it; if you can dream it, you can become it. – William Arthur Ward

If you can imagine it, you can achieve it; if you can dream it, you can become it. – William Arthur Ward

Go confidently in the direction of your dreams. Live the life you have imagined. – Henry David Thoreau

Go confidently in the direction of your dreams. Live the life you have imagined. – Henry David Thoreau

Go confidently in the direction of your dreams. Live the life you have imagined. – Henry David Thoreau

Go confidently in the direction of your dreams. Live the life you have imagined. – Henry David Thoreau

Social Media ContentPlanner

Sunday	Monday	Tuesday	Wednesday	Thursday	Friday	Saturday

Preferred Customers

Name	ID	Phone	Email	Other

Preferred Customers

Name	ID	Phone	Email	Other

Preferred Customers

Name	ID	Phone	Email	Other

Retail Customers

Name	ID	Phone	Email	Other

Distributors

Name	ID	Phone	Email	Other

Name	ID	Phone	Email	Other

Name	ID	Phone	Email	Other

Name	ID	Phone	Email	Other

Contact List

Name	Phone	Email	Contact Dates							

Contact List

Name	Phone	Email	Contact Dates							

Contact List

Name	Phone	Email	Contact Dates							

Contact List

Name	Phone	Email	Contact Dates							

Contact List

Name	Phone	Email	Contact Dates							

Contact List

Name	Phone	Email	Contact Dates							

Contact List

Name	Phone	Email	Contact Dates							

Contact List

Name	Phone	Email	Contact Dates							

Financial freedom is
available to those
who learn about it
and work for it.

~Robert Kiyosaki

Printed in Great Britain
by Amazon

50234076R10088